THE DUNGEON ALPHABET
AN A-TO-Z REFERENCE FOR CLASSIC DUNGEON DESIGN
BY MICHAEL CURTIS

Writer: Michael Curtis • **Editors:** Elizabeth Bauman, Aeryn "Blackdirge" Rudel, Jeff Scifert, Tim Wadzinski
Cover Artist: Erol Otus (color edition), Stefan Poag (gold foil and leather editions) • **Layout:** Peter Bradley, Joseph Goodman, Matt Hildebrand • **Interior Artists:** Jeff Easley, Jim Holloway, Doug Kovacs, William McAusland, Brad McDevitt, Jesse Mohn, Peter Mullen, Russ Nicholson, Erol Otus, Stefan Poag, Jim Roslof, Chad Sergesketter, Chuck Whelon, Mike Wilson, Lutz Winter • **Publisher:** Joseph Goodman

www.goodman-games.com

GOODMAN GAMES

Visit this product's page on DriveThruRPG.com and use the coupon code below to receive a free PDF of this adventure!

10a9b1

NTRODUCTION

BY MICHAEL CURTIS

With fantasy role-playing now approaching its fifth decade of life, the dungeon is no longer the unexplored country it was in the hobby's youth. It has lost something of its wildness and unpredictability as more people have entered the hobby and the number of commercially produced adventures has grown in volume. For many, especially those who've been playing for a while, the dungeon now feels mapped and codified, rendered predictable with familiarity. It is no longer the Wild West or the lawless high seas. The dungeon can still be mysterious and dangerous, but the dew is long off the rose.

It is the purpose of this book to turn the clock back a bit, allowing the dungeon and its delvers a chance to revel in the fun and excitement of a bygone time. It seeks to re-explore a time when the rules weren't quite so well-defined, the sources of inspiration more varied, and the feeling that anything could be found in the dank halls beneath the ground still permeated the air. Collected within these pages are more than forty dungeon tropes, each with a long pedigree in dungeon design. While these tropes are not a comprehensive collection of all the stereotypes associated with the dungeon, they are some of the most commonly encountered by adventurers in their subterranean explorations.

In addition to collecting these classic dungeon elements in one easy-to-use sourcebook, this supplement also attempts look at these overworked characteristics in a somewhat new light, turning the overly-familiar on its ear in order to challenge and entertain even the most hardened and experience fantasy role-player. Whether you're looking to build your first dungeon or your hundred and first, you're bound to find something in these pages that will challenge both the adventurers and, more importantly, their players.

HOW TO USE THIS SUPPLEMENT

Rather than a collection of stats and ready-to-run encounters, this book provides you with the inspiration to create custom designed challenges and interesting locales for your players. As with most things in life, the more work you put into these encounters, the greater the reward you and your players will reap from them. But as most game masters know, even the most well developed encounter is meaningless once the adventurers decide to wander off-script and start pursuing courses of action you hadn't planned on. In times such as these, the game master often has to rely on their own quick thinking to keep the game flowing along smoothly and entertaining for the players.

To help in this matter, each of the entries in this book is accompanied by a random table for the game master to quickly generate something for the characters to confront in the event they wander off the beaten path. When time allows, you can flesh out these encounters to more seamlessly work them into the over-all dungeon canvas, but for the moment, it gives you more to work with than another empty 30' x 30' room.

As one last note, you will see mentioned within these pages that certain items or events have a probability associated with them based on **dungeon level**. This probability is based on the classic "old school" ten level megadungeon complex, with the first level of the dungeon being roughly equal in power to a party of beginning adventurers and the challenge increasing the deeper the party descends. If you intend to use this supplement in the construction of a similar dungeon complex, you can use the dungeon's actual level as the base for determining the probability for these events and encounters. If you're constructing a dungeon for adventurers of higher power, it might be best to use the average power level of the creatures and challenges encountered on each section of the dungeon as the actual **dungeon level** when determining the probability of these events and encounters. Thus, if the very first floor of the dungeon is filled with monsters roughly equal to fourth level in power, treat that level of the dungeon as if it had a **dungeon level** of four rather than one.

IS FOR ALTARS

Blood-stained or radiantly holy, altars are the thresholds separating the mortal from the divine. The site of ghastly rites or benign entreaties, altars lie in grand chambers decorated with religious artifacts and symbols, or in secret places far from the prying eyes of righteous inquisitors. To approach the site of an altar is to walk on ground sacred to a power greater than oneself, a risk that should not be undertaken lightly by adventurers.

Like **Statues**, some altars possess strange powers that can reward the devout or smite the heretical. If the party seeks to thwart the plans of an evil sect, they can be sure that the final conflict will occur at the site of an altar; one surrounded by the suicidal minions and the fell servants of the cult.

HOW TO USE THIS TABLE

To randomly determine what type of altar is found in the dungeon roll a d20 once to determine its appearance. Then either roll a 1d3 or choose a number between 1 and 3 to determine how many accoutrements are present on or near the altar. Roll that number of d20s to determine what is present. For example, the referee rolls a 9 on the first die, indicating the character discovers an altar covered in gold leaf. The referee decides to roll two more d20s to determine what is upon it. Rolls of 13 and 5 show that the altar is covered with an altar cloth and candelabras stand atop it. Since this altar is located on the third level of the dungeon, there is a 30% chance that it bears some special property. A d100 roll of 64 indicates that it has no special powers. Had the referee rolled a 30 or less, another d20 would be rolled to determine those powers.

RANDOM ALTAR GENERATOR

D20 ROLL	APPEARANCE	ACCOUTREMENTS – ROLL 1D3 TIMES	SPECIAL PROPERTIES - 10% CUMULATIVE CHANCE PER DUNGEON LEVEL
1	Crystalline or glass	Large gong	Spells cast while standing beside this altar are at increased power and/or effect.
2	White alabaster	Twin braziers	"Bolt from the blue" does electrical damage to non-believers.
3	Bright scarlet with veins of silver	Statue of god/goddess/saint	Purifies any food or drink placed atop it.
4	Crudely fashioned wood	Drapery hangs behind it	Heals damage to anyone making an offering.
5	Plain stone stained with blood	Covered with altar cloth	Hidden compartment within contains ritual tools and vestments of exquisite make. Worth 1d6x100 gold.
6	Verdigris covered brass	Offering bowl (10% chance per level of 1d100 coins in bowl)	Turns any liquid placed atop it into holy water (50% chance) or vile poison (50% chance).
7	Strong timber bound with metal	Divination tools – joss sticks, augury bones, tiles, etc.	Covers a concealed storage niche, shaft, or stairwell.
8	Rusted iron	Decorated with bas-reliefs of heroes and saints	Imbues believers with protection against normal weapons.
9	Covered in gold leaf (2d10x10 gold value)	Chains attached for securing sacrificial victims	Performs divinations/auguries.
10	Constructed of bones	Sacred texts - 10% chance of clerical scroll present	Transmutes base metals into gold once per week.
11	Fired clay bricks	Studded with gemstones – 80% ornamental/20% semi-precious	Removes/bestows cure on person or object.
12	Pulsating living tissue	Clerical stole	Temporarily enchants items.
13	Iridescent alien metal	Candelabras	Inspires courage/bloodlust in those nearby.
14	Eroded limestone	A humanoid head (artificial or real)	Speaks.
15	Black basalt	Pewter decanter and goblet	Protected by magical barrier which only the faithful may cross.
16	Magically preserved ice	Ceremonial headdress, circlet, or mitre	Places a geas or imparts a quest upon those who touch it.
17	Solid light	Censers or incense holders	Restores all cast spells or prayers.
18	Stone slab held by preserved corpses	Holy/unholy symbol	Resurrects the dead (one-time only).
19	Giant animal covering: turtle shell, beetle carapace, crab exoskeleton, etc.	Ritual scourge/sacrificial knife	Defended by supernatural guardian (elemental, golem, deva, demon/devil, etc.).
20	Natural stone carved in the likeness of a great beast	Bells	Causes alignment change to those who attempt to defile it.

IS ALSO FOR ADVENTURERS

Wherever there are dungeons, there are adventurers, brave, foolish, and greedy, seeking to probe their mysteries and return laden with treasure. Some emerge from the night-black depths victorious, but many are never heard from again. And even though the odds remain stacked against these eccentric bands of would-be heroes and depraved marauders, there is no shortage of fools eager to join their ranks.

Many adventuring bands believe themselves to be de facto owners of their particular dungeon. Having uncovered clues to its existence, spent good gold to outfit themselves and employ hirelings, and journeyed far and endured numerous dangers to reach the delve's forbidding entranceway, they stake their claim upon the site and the riches within, complacent that the dungeon is theirs to plunder until such time as they've pulled every last copper piece from its halls or perished in the attempt. Unfortunately for these companies, they are often not the first to arrive at the dungeon, nor are others inclined to accept their claim on the place after they've entered. This rivalry regularly leads to encounters in the dungeon more dangerous than those with the undercroft's monstrous inhabitants.

Despite the occasional violence when rival adventuring bands meet, a wise party does not begin a meeting with others of their ilk with sword rattling, claims of ownership, or aggressive braggadocio. In the hazardous vocation of dungeon-crawling, allies—especially those that hail from the sunlit lands above—are more valuable than bejeweled idols or hoards of gleaming gold. With so many enemies between them and the dungeon's riches, cooperation is the key to success…unless of course that other band of fortune hunters is not what they seem to be.

A DOZEN UNUSUAL ADVENTURING BANDS

D12 Roll	The adventurers are...

1   Seemingly comatose inside a secured room deep in the dungeon. They do not respond to attempts to wake them, and they are well-equipped and have several bags of treasure with them. Unbeknownst to the PCs, these adventurers are on an astral expedition and their spirits are conducting reconnaissance in the dungeon by viewing its rooms and corridors from another plane of existence. If the PCs attempt to slay these inert rivals, the adventurers become aware of the threat and awaken to fight for their lives. Should the PCs rob their rivals, they make powerful enemies with the ability to observe and ambush them from across planar boundaries. Should the PCs keep watch over the band, they earn formidable allies who possess knowledge of the dungeon's greatest secrets.

2   A group the PCs have met on a former occasion, one that ended with both groups sharing a friendly rivalry and promises to aid one another when they need it. Unfortunately, the other band of adventurers ran afoul of a magical mirror that created evil duplicates of themselves and they died in the encounter. It is these evil twins the party now faces. Careful observation might reveal that the rival adventurers hold weapons in their off-hands or dress in reversed garb.

3   Dressed in armor and clothing long out-of-date and seemingly confused about the state of the dungeon. This party entered the dungeon decades or even centuries ago, but encountered a temporal stasis trap that placed them in a state of suspended hibernation. Recently released after the magical trap finally failed, the party has no idea how much time has elapsed or why the dungeon has changed so suddenly—to them anyway. They may possess useful information about the dungeon's riches and hazards, but this knowledge is also wildly out-of-date. For example, the novice sorcerer they once sought to defeat could now be a powerful lich!

4   A group of scholars on a quest to document dungeon features of historical significance. Consisting of well-meaning but hopelessly naïve historians and their hired bodyguards, the party is mapping, sketching, and recording their finds. To complicate matters, some of the treasure the PCs found has great historic value and the rival party demands they hand it over for the sake of posterity. If the PCs acquiesce, the rival party is willing to share their maps and sketches, giving the heroes insight into a hitherto unexplored section of the dungeon.

5   All dead. Alas for them, the other party has yet to realize they've shuffled off the mortal coil. Powerful magics, a lingering curse, or simply the power of disbelief keeps them going. The party refuses to acknowledge they are dead no matter what evidence is presented and become violent if the PCs continue in their efforts to convince them. Making things worse, their condition is contagious. Every monster the dead party slays in battle also lingers on, but in a more horrific and dangerous undead state. If the PCs reconcile the party with their fate, they are allowed to rest and the undead monsters are destroyed.

6   The PCs themselves but older and better equipped then they currently are. These other PCs are the party's older counterparts who traveled back through time to warn the party of a catastrophe about to befall them in the dungeon. Disturbingly, not all the PCs are present in this other party. The missing members died in the event about to take place. Should the heroes heed their older selves' warning, the catastrophe fails to occur, but this means they have no reason to later come back and warn themselves of it, making this meeting impossible. Referees with a fondness for temporal paradoxes will undoubtedly find ways to drive the players crazy with this encounter.

7   The heirs to the dungeon's original builders. This party recently discovered documents making them the legal owners of the dungeon and came here to evict its current residents and claim their family heirlooms. They're not pleased to discover looters running around in their rightful property and making off with their ancestors' belongings. Despite being at odds with the PCs, they understand the obstacles facing them and are willing to negotiate an agreement to the benefit of both groups. Depending on the dungeon's origins, the party's ancestors might not have been the most goodly-hearted folks, leaving the PCs to wonder if they can trust their new allies.

8   Hopelessly outclassed. The rival party is comprised of individuals that have no right being in the dungeon. They might be idle scions of nobility "slumming" in the dungeon, drunken students whose taproom boasting led them there, or fearful villagers brought into the dungeon by desperate measures. The party's circumstances will determine their reaction to the PCs. The noble scions are condescending, the students are brash and foolhardy, and the villagers are relieved to meet someone better suited to completing their task. Depending on how the PCs respond to the party, they could make devoted friends or vindictive foils.

9   The recently-fired hirelings of yet another party of adventurers. Finding themselves suddenly unemployed in the dungeon depths (for reasons "entirely not our fault"), these former henchmen decided to become adventurers in their own right. They might be driven by greed or by the desire to upstage their former employers. Depending on how they're faring in the dungeon, the party could be eager to find new jobs with the PCs. But seeing how they were abruptly terminated, can they be trusted to carry a torch or 10-foot pole without mucking up the job?

10   From a distant time or place. The party might have angered a powerful alien sorcerer who banished them here or stumbled through a magic portal in a dungeon on a distant planet. Maybe they come from the referee's favorite fantasy novel or perhaps the dungeon is so immense its lowest levels emerge on the opposite side of the world. The party might have objects or powers utterly beyond the PCs' ken and could prove useful if befriended. On the other hand, these rival adventurers might consider the PCs monsters and seek to destroy them from a misguided sense of self-preservation.

11   Artificial constructions sent to learn more about the upper world. A hitherto unknown race dwelling deep within the earth became interested in the surface lands when an adventuring band stumbled into their subterranean realm. After defeating the intruders, the chthonic race created simulacrums based on the interlopers' physical forms and dispatched them to learn more about the world above and those who live there. Their mission might be scientific or a prelude to invasion. The PCs' only clue that all is not what it seems is the party's strange unfamiliarity with common knowledge and customs.

12   "Gone native." As an elven philosopher of yore once wrote, "When you gaze long into the dungeon the dungeon also gazes into you." The party embarked on one too many delves into the dungeon and decided they liked underground life better than that above. This party could be seeking to establish an underworld utopia for themselves and other likeminded adventurers, or they might have gone completely mad and are now as ferocious and monstrous as the creatures they once challenged in the dungeon's depths.

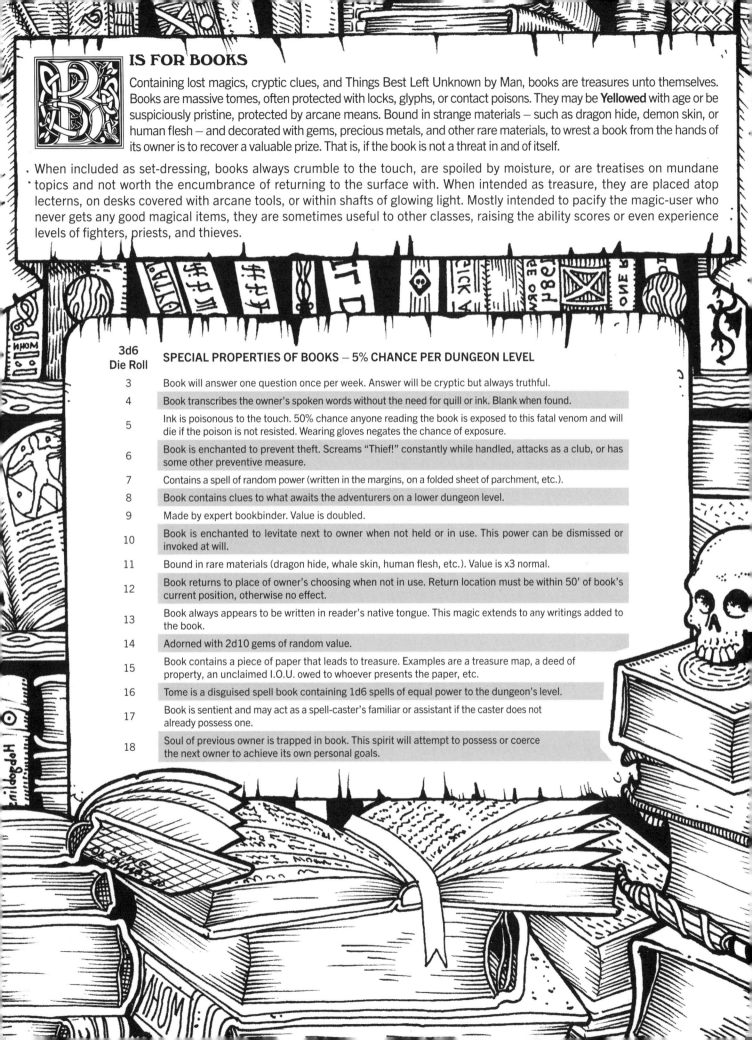

B IS FOR BOOKS

Containing lost magics, cryptic clues, and Things Best Left Unknown by Man, books are treasures unto themselves. Books are massive tomes, often protected with locks, glyphs, or contact poisons. They may be **Yellowed** with age or be suspiciously pristine, protected by arcane means. Bound in strange materials – such as dragon hide, demon skin, or human flesh – and decorated with gems, precious metals, and other rare materials, to wrest a book from the hands of its owner is to recover a valuable prize. That is, if the book is not a threat in and of itself.

When included as set-dressing, books always crumble to the touch, are spoiled by moisture, or are treatises on mundane topics and not worth the encumbrance of returning to the surface with. When intended as treasure, they are placed atop lecterns, on desks covered with arcane tools, or within shafts of glowing light. Mostly intended to pacify the magic-user who never gets any good magical items, they are sometimes useful to other classes, raising the ability scores or even experience levels of fighters, priests, and thieves.

3d6 Die Roll	SPECIAL PROPERTIES OF BOOKS – 5% CHANCE PER DUNGEON LEVEL
3	Book will answer one question once per week. Answer will be cryptic but always truthful.
4	Book transcribes the owner's spoken words without the need for quill or ink. Blank when found.
5	Ink is poisonous to the touch. 50% chance anyone reading the book is exposed to this fatal venom and will die if the poison is not resisted. Wearing gloves negates the chance of exposure.
6	Book is enchanted to prevent theft. Screams "Thief!" constantly while handled, attacks as a club, or has some other preventive measure.
7	Contains a spell of random power (written in the margins, on a folded sheet of parchment, etc.).
8	Book contains clues to what awaits the adventurers on a lower dungeon level.
9	Made by expert bookbinder. Value is doubled.
10	Book is enchanted to levitate next to owner when not held or in use. This power can be dismissed or invoked at will.
11	Bound in rare materials (dragon hide, whale skin, human flesh, etc.). Value is x3 normal.
12	Book returns to place of owner's choosing when not in use. Return location must be within 50' of book's current position, otherwise no effect.
13	Book always appears to be written in reader's native tongue. This magic extends to any writings added to the book.
14	Adorned with 2d10 gems of random value.
15	Book contains a piece of paper that leads to treasure. Examples are a treasure map, a deed of property, an unclaimed I.O.U. owed to whoever presents the paper, etc.
16	Tome is a disguised spell book containing 1d6 spells of equal power to the dungeon's level.
17	Book is sentient and may act as a spell-caster's familiar or assistant if the caster does not already possess one.
18	Soul of previous owner is trapped in book. This spirit will attempt to possess or coerce the next owner to achieve its own personal goals.

ONE HUNDRED BOOK TITLES

D%	Book Title and Author
1	*Things I Have Eaten* by Mortimer Vans Belt
2	*The Vagabond Step-daughter* by Silvias Nati
3	*Eleven Secrets To Be Told* by Der Bluntor
4	*Nightscreams & Whispered Curses* by Reom Fervasz
5	*Comfort, Lunch, & Pipeweed* by Master Thistlebloom
6	*Son, Brother, Lover: The Poems of Erisken of Cullport*
7	*The Apotheosis of Saints* by Father Buckwald Idell
8	*Startled Wren, Happy Heart* by Nessia Wurrel
9	*No Home But Peril* by Quiler Duss
10	*The Dead Amongst Us* by Alligunt Enias – Exorcist General
11	*Oozes of Many Hues and How to Survive Them* by Olli Tenderfeet
12	*The Transmaniacon* by Isosceles Van Damt
13	*Lessons Learned by the Hearth* by Simona Macdoulell
14	*101 Games of Chance* by Eianar Nine-Fingers
15	*The Shine of a Dragon's Scales* by Sir Uln Kurtez
16	*The Ineffable Ledger* by Mikus Pholan
17	*The Knocking Coffin and Other Spine-Tingling Tales* by Teegar Ullen Poh
18	*The Eight Unfinished Sonatas of Maestro Sulk*
19	*Glyphs, Sigils, and Seals* by Antios Spring-Lock
20	*Sand, Wind, and Djinn* by Sajid Hadad
21	*On Wine-Dark Seas: Memoirs of a Sailor* by Cole Swerooth
22	*The Perils of Drink* by Rahyk Veehag
23	*Sixteen Mouths to Feed and Not a Crust of Bread* by Callifax Qool
24	*Roasted Beast and Ale* by Duncan Roughshod
25	*Blood in My Hair* by Essica of Three Wolves Clan
26	*Cold Night* by Ithumm Wynn
27	*I Look to the Stars and Laugh* by Nerrik Utem
28	*We Held the Wall* by Zyllo the Last
29	*River's Sweet Song* by Willomena Coddle
30	*The Dog with Eyes the Size of Flagons* by Bull Jerrillz
31	*The Care and Feeding of Hydras* by Verukian Fell-Monster
32	*The Elixir of Immortality* by Templeton Poole
33	*The Obscure Octavo* by Sebastian Gaunt
34	*A Guide to Cheeses* by Nelvin Cotterpin
35	*The Lineage of Eastern Dukes* by Xull Ullyet, Scribe and Genealogist of the 4th Order
36	*Jokes, Jests, and Grand Guffaws* by Zhekie Fool's Cap
37	*The Rise & Ruin of House Ghud-Hvar* by Rthel Furmalf
38	*Diseases of the Rim Islands* by Brother Qang
39	*Things Said To Me By Sages* by Clesti Allgudd
40	*Clamors & Expeditions* by Silver Eel
41	*A Gentleman's Itch* by Den El-Amor
42	*The Seven Sleepers* by Tolver Half-Hand
43	*Casting Nets at Dreams* by Pente Allozar
44	*Keepsakes and Forget-Me-Nots* by Ilondria Wyverntail
45	*The Rhyme of the Ragged Lich* by Kinwhistle Ootaryes
46	*Preparations and Preservations for the Recently Deceased* by Ghoh Yut-Lenc
47	*The Bruised Book* by Yammod Volt
48	*The Grand Book of Lists* by Junba the Pretty
49	*Fight On, Dog Brothers!* By Tane Macuul
50	*Fat Crows and Widows: A Treatise on War* by Fulymund Erinsen
51	*A Thumb for Every Pie* by Kerrin Rosebush
52	*Growing Up Goblin* by Fthuz IV
53	*At Dawn, I Die* by Edvard Two-Axe
54	*Accusations & Incriminations* by Judge Otiz Gundu
55	*Hold Fast My Fragile Heart* by Hermii Solitariz
56	*What Fools We Be* by Berrows the Lucky
57	*My Toad, My Familiar, My Friend* by Magus Alphonse Stonehurler
58	*The Selected Letters of Archbishop Hy*
59	*War, Theft, and Sorcery* by Tathin Moonlight
60	*Entrails, Clouds & Birds: A Practical Guide to Beginner's Divination* by Ptolus Thutmeses
61	*In Fallow Fields They Lay* by Karin of the Rush River
62	*Lightning Does the Work* by Kolas Letas
63	*The Ram Has Touched the Wall: A Lifetime of Sieges* by Decurion Titus Catullus
64	*My Nights With Kings* by Contessa Inez Imbroglio
65	*Walk With Me, My Friends* by Feo Ilklly
66	*The Lay of Hormir Silverbeard* by Sigurd Redlegs
67	*Holly, Blood, & Mistletoe* by Yenoll Plum, Initiate of the 8th Circle
68	*Hellfires and Abyssal Smoke* by Prior Thomas the Pure
69	*Spaces in Earth: The Story of Neb Gardens* by Ioan Jurrah
70	*My Petals Bloom* by Sorcha Geff
71	*Deadly Glamours of the Unseelie Court* by Reese Fedyth
72	*The Prophecies of the Grand Egg* by Devan Sybill
73	*Herbs of the Night* by Thryvil Clemes
74	*Incantations & Celebrations* by Dithius the Lesser
75	*A Price Too High* by Zeke the Undying
76	*Pages from the Trail* by Rual Sytrik
77	*My Life in the North* by Tobben Rupert
78	*Battered Armor & Shorn Wings* by Kyfael
79	*Schemes of a Fat Merchant* by Mull Thry
80	*Softly, Assassin* by the Anonymous Sell-Blade
81	*The Unified Magic Theorem* by Fabambus Rattletrap
82	*A Primer to Land Management* by Dolliwyv Mepple
83	*What the Nightwatch Saw* by Aggle Hurr
84	*The Wyrm That Gnaws* by Fergus the Thaumaturgist
85	*Blasphemies & Excommunications* by The Grand Heresiarch
86	*Astronomical Phenomenon* by Philus Fetch
87	*Secrets of the Privation Peaks* by Kortze Din Evop
88	*The Bishop Wore Saffron* by Memi Buul
89	*Vulgar Gestures of the Orks* by R'utc Bilegob
90	*The Complete Etchings of Alfonus Dandri*
91	*A Glossary of Dragon Names* by Cyle Ikthan
92	*Art of the Old Empire* by Baron Murthiz Kahyaten
93	*Dwarves' Beard Styles Throughout the Ages* by Gudrun Brubeck
94	*...And We Fear the Worst* by Sister Urabelle St. Grok
95	*Pilgrimage to the City of the Gods* by Evaders Noan
96	*Common Fungi of the Shrieking Caverns* by Nergol Dunwutter
97	*The Philosopher's Conundrum* by Ivar Stuzz
98	*The Master's Art* by Rolo Utes
99	*Lies That Have Saved Me* by Zax Sly-Speaker
00	*Lotsa Humin Storees* by Grunge da Dirty

IS ALSO FOR BATTLES

The sounds of clashing steel and cries of anguish serve as the musical score to dungeon delving. No matter how stealthy, cunning, charismatic, or lucky an adventuring band might be, eventually they must resort to armed combat to achieve their goals. Whether as a pitched skirmish in a gloomy subterranean hallway or the clash of armies in the grand and echoing caverns that perforate the underworld, battles are an inevitable part of the adventuring life.

Fights in the dungeons are as unpredictable as the creatures that dwell there. Surprise—always an element in any armed conflict under the sun or below the earth—is especially important in dungeon battles. It can turn a fight to the party's advantage or doom them to a grisly death. And with so many dungeon-dwelling creatures possessing a wide and unpredictable array of supernatural powers and unusual tactics, it is rare to experience a battle that doesn't include at least one unexpected development before the last foe falls.

While most of these surprise events affect only one side of a conflict, other forces at work in the dungeon can sow confusion and shock in both warring sides, leaving victory in the hands of the group who can recover fastest and turn the unexpected to their advantage. An experienced adventuring band has contingencies for most possible events on the battlefield, be it the arrival of reinforcements, encountering fell magics, or abrupt changes to the terrain. But not even the most veteran of adventuring parties can anticipate all possible cases and must quickly adapt and overcome if they ever wish to see the sun again.

TWENTY UNFORESEEN DEVELOPMENTS DURING A BATTLE

D20 Roll	Suddenly...
1	The flagstones beneath the combatants' feet give way in whole or in part, either plunging them into a yet unexplored part of the dungeon or creating a number of "stepping stones" that must be navigated during the battle.
2	An inexplicable migration of dungeon critters spills onto the battlefield. The migrants could be simple dungeon vermin such as giant centipedes and beetles or more fearsome creatures like oozes, monstrous humanoids, or titanic worms.
3	A mighty blow shatters a crumbling dungeon wall to reveal an unexpected surprise. Hidden in the niche beyond might be a forgotten hoard of treasure, the restless undead forms of entombed prisoners, or a slumbering magical/mechanic construct that stirs to life.
4	Another running battle fights its way onto the scene. These two new opposing forces could be another band of adventurers fighting more of the dungeon's residents, two rival humanoid tribes engaged in a blood feud, or a subterranean predator pursuing its prey.
5	Several of the combatants inexplicably disappear into thin air. After several more minutes, they reappear unharmed but bewildered. Once the fight is over, the surviving fighters who vanished tell a strange tale of being spirited away by powerful supernatural entities who forced them to perform bizarre tasks or recount being strapped down while weird, grey-skinned figures enacted uncomfortable scientific tests upon them.
6	One of the party's monstrous opponents stares intently at a member and screams out, "Father?!" Is this as cunning ploy or the PC's shameful past coming back to haunt him?
7	Both sides find themselves abruptly immobilized in mid-conflict. As they watch helplessly, a pair of beings walks onto the battlefield, deep in conversation. They pay scant interest to the combatants as they engage in a philosophical debate about the nature of good and evil. The debaters might be a duo of mortal wizards, an angel and a demon, or a pair of godlings wandering the material world. After they walk off the battlefield, the fighters can move once again.
8	The magical energies wielded by both sides' spells combine to produce unnatural meteorological effects. A rain of fish pelts the combatants, a windstorm buffets the battlefield, or a severe snowfall covers the warring parties. Further spells cast during the battle intensify the bizarre weather.
9	A schism erupts within the opponent's ranks. This mutiny might be caused by rival factions deciding this to be the perfect moment to eliminate their opposite numbers, troops pressed into service rebelling against their masters, or the result of a hidden benefactor's magical influence to rescue the party from an overwhelming force.
10	A chance blow releases something best left contained. A club smashes a backpack filled with potions, creating unpredictable results when the volatile substances are mixed; a flask of oil shatters, drenching its owner in combustible liquid; or a lucky blow breaches the ancient brass bottle the party carries, freeing the powerful and angry efreeti trapped within!
11	A torrent of water rushes into the area, threatening all sides with drowning. The flood might be the result of a ruptured dam somewhere else in the dungeon, a flash flood in the lands above, or a malfunctioning magical item that taps into the Elemental Plane of Water.
12	The bodies of slain combatants rise as undead creatures and attack both sides. This abrupt animation might be the result of a bored deity or a lurking necromancer, or powered by a mystical artifact carried unwittingly by one of the combatants.
13	Other intelligent residents of the dungeon turn up to watch the battle. They stand on the sidelines howling encouragement and insults while placing wagers with one another regarding the outcome. If the party is victorious and wins a prestigious spectator large sums of gold, they might gain an unexpected benefactor within the dungeon.
14	The corpses of dead opponents attract the mindless monsters that serve as the dungeon's cleaning crew. These beasts pay no notice to the livelier combatants, choosing to concentrate their attentions on the easy pickings that litter the battlefield. The battle becomes increasingly difficult as the fighters must navigate around or over flesh-eating oozes, puddings, or other scavenging monsters.
15	The opposing side stops fighting and parleys for a cease of hostilities so they might observe their daily religious ceremony. If the PCs rebuff the request and continue to attack, their opponents' god takes an interest in the battle and divinely assists his/her/its worshipers against their heretical opponents.
16	A brazier, lamp, or torch is knocked over, setting alight inflammable materials on or next to the battlefield. Depending on the ignited material, the killing field might turn into a raging inferno or merely become occluded by thick smoke. Intelligent opponents might flee the field, but those inspired by zealotry or defending their lairs fight more ferociously to keep the PCs from escaping or to slay their opponents swiftly so they can extinguish the blaze.
17	The party's opponents are revealed to be entirely different creatures than the PCs believed them to be. The fearsome orcs are actually bandits wearing costumes as part of their criminal scheming; the skeletons are all living humanoids that drank from a pool which turned their skin and organs invisible; or a giant lizard is truly a dragon that lost its wings to an enchanted blade.
18	Time slips, throwing chronological order askew. The battle may "reset" to the beginning, causing slain creatures to return to life, accelerate or decelerate the actions of one side, or change the order in which the combatants act. This effect might be the result of magical phenomenon or an unexpected glitch in the time-space continuum. All parties are affected by it and no explanation may ever be discovered for the time slip.
19	The opposing side transforms into different creatures. Perhaps the party was fighting lycanthropes who suddenly change form or the enemy possesses magical items that polymorph them into unexpected creatures. In extreme cases, an unknown participant, perhaps a chaos demon or mischievous godling, shape-changes both sides into one another's guises.
20	The battlefield changes dramatically. Walls suddenly appear, the combatants are teleported to a new location, or they are thrown onto a different world or plane. Unbeknownst to either side, their fight activated a slumbering magical item or a contingency spell that chose the particular moment of their battle to take effect.

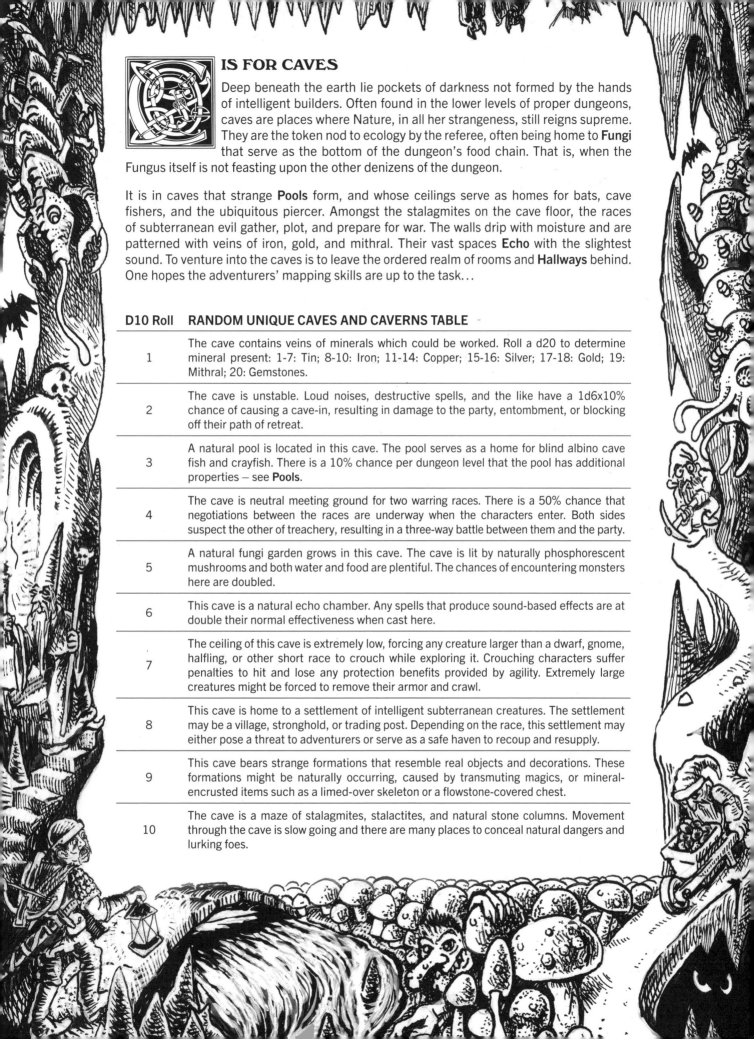

IS FOR CAVES

Deep beneath the earth lie pockets of darkness not formed by the hands of intelligent builders. Often found in the lower levels of proper dungeons, caves are places where Nature, in all her strangeness, still reigns supreme. They are the token nod to ecology by the referee, often being home to **Fungi** that serve as the bottom of the dungeon's food chain. That is, when the Fungus itself is not feasting upon the other denizens of the dungeon.

It is in caves that strange **Pools** form, and whose ceilings serve as homes for bats, cave fishers, and the ubiquitous piercer. Amongst the stalagmites on the cave floor, the races of subterranean evil gather, plot, and prepare for war. The walls drip with moisture and are patterned with veins of iron, gold, and mithral. Their vast spaces **Echo** with the slightest sound. To venture into the caves is to leave the ordered realm of rooms and **Hallways** behind. One hopes the adventurers' mapping skills are up to the task…

D10 Roll	RANDOM UNIQUE CAVES AND CAVERNS TABLE
1	The cave contains veins of minerals which could be worked. Roll a d20 to determine mineral present: 1-7: Tin; 8-10: Iron; 11-14: Copper; 15-16: Silver; 17-18: Gold; 19: Mithral; 20: Gemstones.
2	The cave is unstable. Loud noises, destructive spells, and the like have a 1d6x10% chance of causing a cave-in, resulting in damage to the party, entombment, or blocking off their path of retreat.
3	A natural pool is located in this cave. The pool serves as a home for blind albino cave fish and crayfish. There is a 10% chance per dungeon level that the pool has additional properties – see **Pools**.
4	The cave is neutral meeting ground for two warring races. There is a 50% chance that negotiations between the races are underway when the characters enter. Both sides suspect the other of treachery, resulting in a three-way battle between them and the party.
5	A natural fungi garden grows in this cave. The cave is lit by naturally phosphorescent mushrooms and both water and food are plentiful. The chances of encountering monsters here are doubled.
6	This cave is a natural echo chamber. Any spells that produce sound-based effects are at double their normal effectiveness when cast here.
7	The ceiling of this cave is extremely low, forcing any creature larger than a dwarf, gnome, halfling, or other short race to crouch while exploring it. Crouching characters suffer penalties to hit and lose any protection benefits provided by agility. Extremely large creatures might be forced to remove their armor and crawl.
8	This cave is home to a settlement of intelligent subterranean creatures. The settlement may be a village, stronghold, or trading post. Depending on the race, this settlement may either pose a threat to adventurers or serve as a safe haven to recoup and resupply.
9	This cave bears strange formations that resemble real objects and decorations. These formations might be naturally occurring, caused by transmuting magics, or mineral-encrusted items such as a limed-over skeleton or a flowstone-covered chest.
10	The cave is a maze of stalagmites, stalactites, and natural stone columns. Movement through the cave is slow going and there are many places to conceal natural dangers and lurking foes.

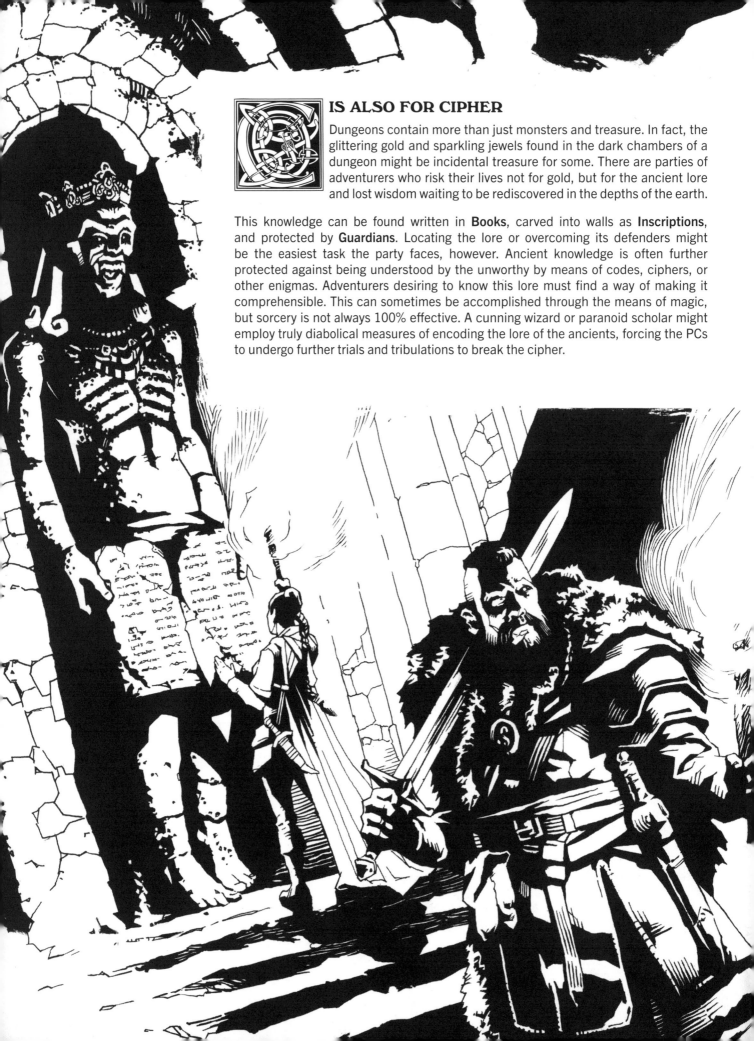

IS ALSO FOR CIPHER

Dungeons contain more than just monsters and treasure. In fact, the glittering gold and sparkling jewels found in the dark chambers of a dungeon might be incidental treasure for some. There are parties of adventurers who risk their lives not for gold, but for the ancient lore and lost wisdom waiting to be rediscovered in the depths of the earth.

This knowledge can be found written in **Books**, carved into walls as **Inscriptions**, and protected by **Guardians**. Locating the lore or overcoming its defenders might be the easiest task the party faces, however. Ancient knowledge is often further protected against being understood by the unworthy by means of codes, ciphers, or other enigmas. Adventurers desiring to know this lore must find a way of making it comprehensible. This can sometimes be accomplished through the means of magic, but sorcery is not always 100% effective. A cunning wizard or paranoid scholar might employ truly diabolical measures of encoding the lore of the ancients, forcing the PCs to undergo further trials and tribulations to break the cipher.

D10 Roll	TEN CIPHERS TO CONFOUND THE PARTY
1	An odd, clearly out of place word is discovered carved into a statue or scrawled on a dungeon wall. Another is found soon thereafter. There are 2d4 of these words scattered about the dungeon, and if all are found and placed in the proper sequence, a code capable of opening an otherwise impenetrable dungeon door is revealed.
2	A common type of humanoid in the dungeon (goblins, kobolds, orcs, gnomes, etc.) speaks a strange local dialect of their species' language, making it difficult to comprehend what they're saying—even by PCs fluent in that species' tongue. The game master should use some linguistic trick when role-playing these monsters, speaking in "pig Latin," talking backwards, phrasing sentences in a bizarre, Yoda-like fashion, or otherwise complicating their speech to make the players themselves figure out what the monsters are saying.
3	An important, but not essential, bit of lore is discovered in the dungeon, written in a magical script that cannot be understood except through the use of translation spells. However, when this writing is translated, the words, although now recognizable, form no sensible message. The lore is further protected by a code unaffected by the spell's magic. The players will have to locate the key to decipher the code or break it themselves to benefit from the encrypted wisdom.
4	The party discovers a powerful magical item, such as the staff of an arch-magi or an artifact of old. Unfortunately, the command word needed to activate the object and use its immense power is scrambled, either purposely or by accident. The PCs have to piece together the proper order of the letters. Complicating matters, each time they attempt to invoke the item's power using a word formed by an incorrect arrangement of letters, the magical item produces an unpredictable effect and wastes one of its charges.
5	A code is found written on a piece of paper or a small tablet with no means to decipher it. However, a curious skull bearing strange glyphs and bizarre ornamentation is found nearby. A slot, large enough for the object the cipher is written upon to pass through, is present in the skull's top. If the cipher-bearing object is placed into the slot and a spell that allows communication with the dead is cast upon the cranium, it begins jabbering away, translating the cipher into the PCs' normal language.
6	A powerful spell or ancient piece of lore is written on a single continuous piece of fabric. Unfortunately, this piece of fabric is being used as the wrappings of an evil and powerful mummy in the dungeon. The party must not only defeat the mummy in order to unwrap it and gain the lore they seek but must do so in a way as to keep the knowledge from being damaged. This means no fireballs or flaming oil, and slashing the undead creature to pieces with sharp swords threatens to destroy or at least scramble the message. Even vials of holy water could cause the ancient inks to run and the lore or spell to be lost forever. The party will have to be smart to defeat the undead creature and still recover the lore.
7	The party discovers a seemingly incomplete message or partial code. Despite their best efforts, they cannot discern its meaning. The reason: part of the message or code is written in invisible letters that can only be seen with certain abnormal forms of vision. Infravision or darkvision might be all that's necessary to decode it if the party is comprised entirely of humans, but a mixed species group might need the help of a more exotic creature or individual: the sight of a fairy, the gaze of a beholder, or the petrifying vision of a medusa could be necessary to see the invisible letters. How does the party convince this creature to help them?
8	A magic cipher is only legible to one on the cusp of death. In order to correctly translate the writing, it must be viewed by one whose spirit is slipping free of their mortal body. The writing can be read by someone with zero hit points or fewer (depending on your game system), glimpsed during an out-of-body experience. Now, who's willing to be stabbed by their fellow adventurers to break the code?
9	The message isn't written in letters but conveyed via another form of sensory input: smell, sound, or taste, for example. The knowledge might be written as musical notation and only by playing the notes does the lore suddenly make itself known to the listener as if by sudden enlightenment. Or perhaps an array of sealed jars containing fragrant herbs or flowers needs to be opened and sniffed in the proper order (which is written on some other piece of paper elsewhere in the dungeon) to learn the knowledge the party seeks.
10	The party finds the knowledge they're after only to discover it's written in an unbreakable code, one whose key was lost long ago to a fire, war or other mishap. In order to decipher the information, they must travel back in time before the key was lost. This might result in them delving into the same dungeon they're currently exploring but at a time when it was occupied by far different inhabitants. The game master can reuse the same dungeon map, but replace its contents with entirely new ones, ones more appropriate for the dungeon's purpose back when the code key still existed.

IS ALSO FOR CRYPTS

Subterranean sepulchers lie forgotten in the lightless depths beneath the earth. Some of these final resting places were constructed far from the sun to prevent tomb robbers from plundering their contents. Others, however, were excavated in the darkness because what they housed was antithetical to goodness and light. As the adventuring party approaches the crypt's door, its seals still intact, they wonder which of the two they're about to enter.

Crypts are often unsurprisingly the abode of the **Undead.** Stirred by curses, necromantic power, or their own undying hate, the occupants of the crypt rise from their biers and stalk the dusty, dark interiors of their tombs. Some wander mindlessly, stirred to action only when their crypt is breached by intruders. Yet other undead occupants retain a spark of their living minds and use their final resting place as a base of operations, a sanctum from which to launch revenge or conquest against the living. These intelligent undead often amplify their crypt's existing defenses against tomb robbers with other undead guardians and cunning traps.

Despite the risks of its restless occupants, crypts are tantalizing targets for adventurers. Besides the often plentiful and valuable grave goods found inside the tombs, the sepulchers are also repositories for lost magical knowledge such as spells and potion formulas, as well as historical lore pertinent to problems plaguing the current era. If the crypt's defenders can be overcome, treasures both intellectual and material await the victors.

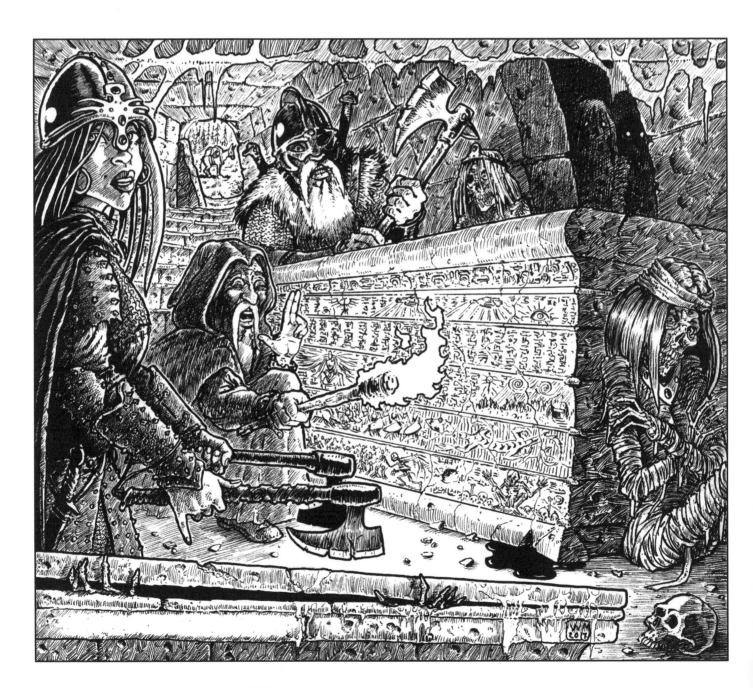

A DOZEN CREEPY CRYPTS

D12 Roll	The crypt is…
1	Located beneath the palace of a great king. An old potentate was buried with a piece of lore the king needs to overcome some threat to the kingdom, a danger the old king defeated in his day. But the crypt is in the deepest, darkest reaches beneath the palace and said to be haunted by ghosts and powerful curses. The king is looking for adventurers to locate and plunder it.
2	A vast necropolis created to honor the power of Death. According to an ancient compact made by the crypt's creator and Death itself, once the mausoleum is filled, Death will allow one victim it has claimed down the eons to return to the world of the living. Depending on who would be resurrected, the party might find themselves either trying to fill the crypt's remaining niches or prevent one final body from being interred.
3	A crude affair created by a party of adventurers to house the mortal remains of the various henchmen and hirelings who died helping their explorations of the dungeon. The morale of any living hirelings, even those not working for that adventuring group, is negatively affected after discovering the ad-hoc tomb.
4	The repository of the mortal remains of an unusual creature. It might be a dragon's tomb; a mausoleum housing countless mummified animals such as cats, dogs, baboons, or crocodiles; a sepulcher for a skeletal whale far from the ocean; or other curious occupants. The mystery of how they got there and why the crypt was constructed will perplex the adventurers for many game sessions.
5	Protected by inscribed magical symbols intended to keep the undead from arising within the tomb. The glyphs drain away necromantic energy and prevent that dark power from pooling. This power could have beneficial side-effects such as healing the living with life-rich magic, or detrimental results like syphoning away the souls of creatures who spend too much time within the crypt.
6	Instilled with a magical cooling system to keep the bodies from decaying. Ice and rime cover every surface, and the interred remains appear to be sleeping beneath a blanket of frost. Rather than undead, the crypt is home to several cold-loving species, drawn to the crypt by its frigid atmosphere.
7	The final resting place of venerated objects rather than people. It houses old books too brittle and worn to be rebound, swords too pitted and rusty to hold an edge, or aged religious icons too shabby for regular use but too holy to destroy. Devout individuals related to the objects (librarians for the books, for example) are interred along with the item to protect the tomb after death.
8	Filled with magical illusions of the interred occupant(s) as they were in life. The images move about, performing everyday tasks as they did while alive. Not all the images are illusions, however. One might be the undead occupant in ghostly or life-like physical form, waiting to ambush intruders.
9	The tomb of a dead pharaoh, but one whose name has been removed from all the inscriptions within it by jealous or hateful successors. The desecration has given rise to a potent undead creature, but if its name is properly restored, it grants a blessing or wish to those who aid it.
10	Filled with rich-seeming treasures. Unfortunately, these are all faux treasures designed to serve the crypt's occupant in the afterlife and possess no real world value.
11	Home to a functioning portal to the afterlife. Unfortunately, it's a one-way portal.
12	Not yet in use. The tomb has been prepared for the demise of some powerful creature or leader, but the individual still lives. All the traps are activated, however, to protect the tomb until it's needed.

IS FOR DOORS

Barriers between the ordered lands of light above and the shrouded halls of evil below, doors are often as dangerous as what lies behind them. Home of **Traps** and ear seekers alike, doors are never to be trusted. They are stubborn to open and quick to close once the party has passed through. The door's thickness obscures the sounds of those who lurk behind them, clouding their numbers even when their gibbering tongues can be perceived.

Doors come in many forms, but iron bound wood are the most common, usually swollen with the moisture of many years. A door that opens easily is a sign of danger. Either it is used regularly by the creatures within, indicating that many monsters lie just ahead, or it is an invitation to visit the hungry denizens or traps that lay behind it.

TWENTY INTERESTING DUNGEON DOORS

D20 Roll	
1	Door cannot be completely closed due to warped hinges, swollen with moisture, crooked frame, etc.
2	Door spiked from inside by previous adventurers.
3	Crudely written sign hangs from door: "Knock, you yam-heads!," "Back in 5 minutes," "If you can read this, it's too late…," etc.
4	Door has been battered down and crudely repaired.
5	Door is one-way only.
6	False door. True entrance is through a nearby secret door.
7	Peephole set in door.
8	Small barred window set in door.
9	Animal skin/humanoid hide/skulls/severed limbs nailed to door.
10	Door appears to be a mirror. Opens as a secret door.
11	Door is transparent on opposite side.
12	Door falls upon anyone who attempts to open it.
13	Door is intelligent and will not let anyone pass without proper password, answering a riddle, performing some minor entertainment to amuse it, etc.
14	Door is alarmed by magical or mundane means.
15	Door is of abnormal size (small or huge) or shape (triangular/hexagonal/round, etc.).
16	Door is of a strange material (glass, force, bone, solid fire, etc.).
17	Door is sealed with lead and covered with magical inscriptions warning of danger beyond.
18	Door is actually a disguised monster.
19	Door is water- or air- tight. Danger results from opening it.
20	Door is of an unusual nature – turnstile, pressure door, vault door, revolving door, etc.

D IS ALSO FOR DRAGONS

In the dim past, dragons and dungeons were inescapably linked. Every adventurer worth his salt knew that sooner or later his subterranean exploits would lead him into a dragon's den. The great wyrms claimed parts of the dungeon as their own, squeezing their bulky, scaly forms into the narrow halls and low-ceilinged chambers without fear of being challenged by the delve's other inhabitants. Dungeons, especially their lowest levels, were unquestionably dragon country.

At some point, however, this changed and adventurers no longer feared to find dragons at home deep within the earth. After all, such titanic beasts obviously needed much larger accommodations with plentiful food sources and room to store their vast hoards, and adventuring bands began to identify mountain peaks, great glaciers, and thorny forests as the homes of dragons. Unfortunately for these folks, rationality seldom has a place in the undercroft and logic makes for a poor shield against the burning breath of an unexpectedly encountered wyrm in the depths of the earth.

Wise adventurers learn to dismiss no possibilities when it comes to dragons, for they are a long-lived and cunning species. The smartest of dragons use the expectations of others to their benefit, and it is often these same dragons that lair in dungeons. A dungeon's confined spaces can be used to the wyrm's advantage, especially when the dragon can change shape or cast spells to ease its passage through tight dungeon corridors. Particularly dangerous are those rare dragons who are unique creatures, perhaps the last or first of their kind. A dungeon makes fine lair for a dragon with many enemies or who seeks to remain a myth until it chooses to reveal itself. Woe unto the party of adventurers who discovers this clandestine drake, for their deaths are the sole means by which the dragon can keep its existence secret.

FIFTEEN FEARSOME DUNGEON-DWELLING DRAGONS

2D8 Roll	The dragon is...
2	Imprisoned within the dungeon. Brought here centuries ago as a bound servant to a great mage, the dragon was formerly encased in a magical sphere that kept it a reduced size. When the mage released it to do battle with his enemies, the dragon was then abandoned and could not escape through the level's available exits. Since that time, it has shaped its dungeon lair to best accommodate its bulk but still seeks freedom. The party who could provide such an escape would be greatly rewarded.
3	A rare type or color. Perhaps it is the last of its kind, its brethren slain in some ancient war, or maybe it is a unique specimen, the result of forbidden mating between two diverse dragon species that resulted in a never-before-seen progeny. In either case, the dragon hides within the dungeon, ruling its level and scheming to gain power and magic so it can hold its own against the enemies that will ultimately challenge it once it reveals itself to the rest of dragonkind.
4	Evolved to subterranean habitats. This dragon is one of a species forced into the bowels of the earth by ancient events. Since that time, these dragons evolved to better fit into the chthonic world. Their wings have become vestigial or vanished completely. Their scales are now white from lack of sun, and the original species is impossible to tell. Their bodies are sinuous and their legs low-slung and short to better squeeze into narrow spaces. These adaptations and familiarity with the dark places beneath the earth make them terrifying opponents to engage in the snaking, cramped halls of the dungeon.
5	A fossil. Although the rest of the dungeon's residents claim a portion of the dungeon is held by a fierce, subterranean wyrm, they've never seen it for themselves. After avoiding that part of the dungeon because their forefathers warned them never to disturb the dragon that dwelled there, they have no idea that the dragon succumbed to illness or despair long ago and is now naught but bones amidst gleaming gold. Perhaps a small number of the dungeon's inhabitants have learned the truth and perpetuate the myth of the dragon while using its feared lair and the contents therein to their own advantage.
6	A shape-changer. Through either ownership of a magical item or an innate ability, the dragon can alter its form to better exist within the dungeon's strict confines. It transforms to leave its lair, venturing to the surface to hunt and mate, and then returns via secret passages to its secure den. Some shape-changing dragons maintain alter-egos within the dungeon, interacting with other inhabitants in much different personas, gathering information, and sowing discord to protect themselves from interlopers.
7	A construct. Although dragon-like in form, the wyrm is actually an artificial life form crafted by a long-dead creator. As a construct, it requires none of the biological necessities a living dragon needs and is content to dwell entirely within the dungeon proper, engaged in whatever ineffable task its master built it for. A few such constructs have developed "artificial intelligence" and in their long existences have come to believe they are in fact dragons and behave in a manner they deem appropriate for their scaly guise.
8	Hibernating. Centuries or perhaps millennia ago the dragon lay down to enter one of the eon-long sleeps for which their kind is known. As time passed, the dungeon formed around or above the dragon, imprisoning it. Certain safeguards, either natural or designed, have kept the wyrm from being slain in its slumber, and the other dungeon residents give it a wide berth for fear of waking it and bringing doom down upon their heads. Of course, incautious and brazen adventurers are perfect candidates for doing just that, and the beast will wake hungry, angry, and confounded about the events that have occurred during its long doze.
9	Undead. The great dragon has slipped beyond the bounds of life, but through magic or sheer will persists in an undead state. As an undead beast, it no longer requires food (although still enjoys the crunch of bones and splash of blood between its jaws), and its decayed form and tattered wings make travel through the dungeon halls easy. Such a dread wyrm would be a potent ally for evil-bent creatures or may possess lore long forgotten by those in the sunlit lands above. However, its great age and abnormal abilities make it a formidable opponent for anyone seeking to use it to their own ends.
10	Recently hatched. Some wyrms go to great lengths to protect their offspring, and a dragon with the ability to change its form might choose to lay a clutch of eggs in the inaccessible depths of a dungeon. There, the hatchlings would be safe from the predation of other dragons who often engage in cannibalism and genocide to keep their territories secure and limit potential threats to their domains. Unfortunately for adventurers seeking an easy dragon-hide trophy, some species of dragons lay multiple eggs at a time, and these creatures hatch to form writhing snarls of young, hungry wyrmlings.
11	Wounded. The dragon was injured in combat or contracted a rare dragon affliction and has retreated into the dungeon to nurse its wounds, secure in the knowledge that it is unlikely to be disturbed while it recovers. The good news for adventurers who accidentally encounter it is that the dragon is not at full strength and not nearly as formidable as it might normally be. The bad news is that it has little in the way of material wealth, having been forced to abandon its hoard when it fled to the dungeon. However, the dragon might be predisposed to sharing some of its wealth if the party offers healing and agrees to assist it in gaining revenge or retaking its lair.
12	Of below-average size. Whether through a magical mishap or simply weak genes, the dragon is much smaller than others of its species. Although the dragon possesses all the normal powers and capabilities of a typical dragon of its kind, its reduced size places it at a disadvantage when challenging other dragons for territory and mates. Because of this, the dwarf dragon is forced to dwell in the dungeon where its size is a benefit. Such abnormally-sized dragons are likely to suffer from a "Napoleon complex," making it aggressive and itching for a fight when encountered.
13	A dream dragon. This dragon is not flesh and blood but a manifestation of the dungeon inhabitants' belief that a dragon dwells amongst them. Their collective expectation that a dragon shares the dungeon has caused a semi-solid wyrm to coalesce in the subterranean halls with all the abilities and danger that accompany a real dragon. As it is not a living creature, it cannot be slain in a traditional manner and always reforms so long as the dungeon's creatures continue to unfailingly believe the dragon is real.
14	A "god." The dragon once entered the dungeon for another purpose (roll randomly on the chart or create your own), but became a divine figure in the eyes of other dungeon monsters. With a congregation providing its every need, the dragon sees no reason to depart its subterranean heaven and has grown fat and content in the dark—so fat that leaving the dungeon is no longer an option. Despite his ungainly size and sense of self-importance, this "god" remains a potent threat if its cult is threatened or heretics dare attack its own divine corpus.
15	Searching for something. The dragon only recently entered the dungeon and is extremely displeased with having to do so. Nevertheless, the wyrm must risk the cramped spaces to acquire an item or treasure it desperately seeks. It wishes nothing more than to find its prize and depart the dungeon as quickly as possible. If the PCs have entered the dungeon in search of their own magical trinket or object of vast wealth, the dragon likely seeks the same and stands as an obstacle that must be overcome.
16	A hoax. Despite rumors of a dragon's presence in the dungeon and evidence supporting these legends (a loose scale, fire-blackened stone, great claw marks, etc.), the feared wyrm does not actually exist. The rumors and evidence are all the work of another non-draconic creature hiding behind a ruse. The creature may wish to be left alone and believes a dragon's lair is likely to be avoided, or it might have more esoteric reasons for masquerading as a wyrm. Perhaps it hopes to lure a true dragon to its lair as part of a crafty or outlandishly mad scheme.

IS FOR ECHOES

The stone walls, floors, and ceilings of the dungeon play tricks with noise and sound. The voices of the party ring all too loud in vast chambers, and the tread of their booted feet carries much too far down the **Hallways**, alerting those who live within. Echoes muddy the sounds of monsters, causing their numbers to sound greater or lesser than are actually present. They amplify the sounds of a driven iron spike or the tapping of a 10' pole, summoning wandering monsters to dinner. An astute dwarf might be able to judge the size of a cave by the echoes reverberating within, but certain creatures use those same echoes to track down their prey.

D6 Roll	SIX WAYS TO USE ECHOES
1	The party discovers a room that, through accident or design, functions as a "whispering gallery," allowing them to overhear the conversations and actions of creatures in another section of the dungeon. This "whispering gallery" works in both directions, so a loud or incautious party will alert those denizens to their own presence and activities.
2	The noises caused by the party's explorations are repeated from deeper within the complex. The delay that occurs between the original action and the echo is too long to be a naturally occurring phenomenon. Something is purposely mimicking them. These echoes might be a semi-intelligent creature playing a "game," or it might be a gambit employed by more intelligent foes seeking to lure the party into an ambush or trap.
3	At a regular interval (once an hour or twice a day, for example), a loud growling sound echoes through the dungeon hallways. This noise could be the sound that heralds the regular feeding of some large creature by its owners, or it might be caused by a lift or elevator room that makes regular stops on this dungeon level.
4	A large chamber or vast cavern echoes back the characters' conversations. Incredibly, the echoes are not in the original language spoken. Instead, the party hears their conversation repeated in dwarven, goblin, or a long-dead language. The content remains the same, only the language has changed.
5	Strange veins of an unknown mineral wind their way through the stone walls of the dungeon. This mineral, known as chimestone, acts as a natural telegraph that transmits the sound of an object striking the exposed mineral along the entire vein. Some subterranean races use these veins as method of communicating between long distances underground by tapping out a form of Morse Code on the vein, which is picked up by those dwelling at the opposite end.
6	The architecture of the dungeon causes echoes to be distorted, making it difficult to gauge the number of creatures making noise within its halls. The effect differs from section to section. In some areas, it mutes the sounds of the inhabitants, making it seem as if only half the number of creatures is present. In other section, it amplifies the noise made by the inhabitants, making five kobolds sound like twenty, or small insects sound like their giant counterparts.

IS ALSO FOR ENTRANCES

Before the doughty adventurer can reap the dungeon's spoils and challenge its monstrous inhabitants, she must first cross the threshold into the underworld. The sun is behind her and the darkness of the subterranean realm embraced. It is time to enter the dungeon proper, sword and torch in hand.

Taverngoers who've only dreamed of venturing into the sunless places under the earth envision the dungeon's entrance as a dark hole with stairs leading down into it. In many cases, this imagining is indeed correct. Experience adventurers, however, know that dungeon entrances are as varied as the monsters who inhabit them. Some entryways are blatant, while others are secret. There are entrances that open only at certain times of the year or only when a specific key is held. Sometimes, half the adventure is simply finding that the entrance exists in the first place!

While dungeon exploration cannot proceed without knowing where its entrance lies and how to access it, more than a few adventurers have rued the day they discovered the means to descend into the underworld. Or they would have, had they survived long enough in the dungeon to do so...

TWENTY ENTICING ENTRANCES

D20	The entrance is...
1	A winding stairway hidden among ruins of the past.
2	A natural cave mouth with eldritch symbols inscribed around its rim.
3	A hollow tree with a ladder leading downwards.
4	A pair of glowing pillars with heat distortion between them. Stepping into the waving air causes the traveler to appear inside the dungeon.
5	Hidden inside a magical item. Touching the pommel of a sword or the gemstone on a staff transports the person making contact to the dungeon.
6	Accessible only in dreams. To reach it the first time, the adventurer must quest to find a depiction of the entryway in an ancient carving, old book, or similar means of replicating it. Only then, after seeing the depiction, can they hope to dream of the entrance.
7	A crumbling mine adit standing forgotten in the hills.
8	At the bottom of a lake. The lake either drains at certain times of the year, allowing access, or powerful magic keeps the waters out when the dungeon entrance is opened.
9	Under the paw of a massive stone sphinx deep in the desert.
10	The corked mouth of an ancient bottle or jar. Unstopping the container whisks the opener and all nearby into the dungeon.
11	In the royal crypts, the thieves' guild's main vault, under the main temple of the god of war, or another location where it will be an adventure just reaching the dungeon's entrance!
12	Among the flames of an eternal fire. The adventurers will have to either risk the fire or find magic to protect them from the heat.
13	Part of an enchanted painting that teleports anyone gazing up at the work to the dungeon.
14	Visible in a reflective surface such as a mirror or a still pond. The adventurers must walk in reverse towards the entrance while staring at the reflection in order to enter the dungeon.
15	Found at the end of the secret paths of cats. The adventurers must convince a feline to allow them to follow it along the routes known only to that species. The cat desires something in return.
16	Among the shadows cast when an enchanted lantern is lit. Like a piece in a performance of shadow play, the doorway to the dungeon then appears.
17	Shut until a certain time or event takes place. This might be the birthday of the dungeon's creator, a celestial concordance, a holiday, the death of a powerful magi, or similar circumstance. How long the entrance remains open is left to the game master's potentially devious imagination.
18	One-way. Once a creature passes through, they cannot exit through that access point. The entrance might be sealed behind them by a magical barrier, lack means to open from inside the dungeon, or vanish completely.
19	Opened only with a sacrifice of some kind. This sacrifice might be blood, magical power, physical traits, undertaking a geas, swearing to an oath, or a similar cost extracted from the one seeking entry.
20	A transformative portal. All creatures passing through it must resist magic or undergo some form of physical change. They might shrink in size, swap minds, change gender or race, or otherwise become other than normal. These changes might be temporary or they may only be reversed if the party finds some special object or location within the dungeon itself.

IS FOR FUNGI

Loathsome growths birthed in the fetid environment of the dungeon, fungi are both malevolent and benign, but always unsettling. From gigantic toadstools to patches of tiny mushrooms, fungi in the dungeon are more treacherous than their upper world counterparts. Sometimes they are edible, if the party has run out of rations, but more commonly it is the fungi that does the eating, infecting the unwary with fatal, alien growths. Not even keeping one's distance is protection against this unnatural life, as some fungi can uproot themselves to walk freely within the dank confines of the dungeon. Mostly unintelligent, driven only by the need to reproduce themselves in the flesh of the adventurer, they cannot be parleyed with, bribed, or distracted by food or treasure. Even when intelligent, the drives and motivations of fungi are too alien to be easily comprehended.

EIGHT STRANGE FORMS OF FUNGUS

D8 Roll

1 Fungi are harmless but expel spores that have a hallucinogenic effect on surface races. Any character failing to resist these spores becomes confused and may wander off, attack inanimate objects, attack other party members, sit motionless for hours, or otherwise act irrationally while under the spores' influence.

2 If eaten, the fungi convey strange properties on the character. The character might find himself growing to gigantic size, glowing in the dark, able to comprehend any spoken language, healed of damage, able to see in darkness or detect invisible creatures, or able to breathe underwater.

3 If eaten, the fungus begins to infect the eater, turning his body into a spongy mass. The effect takes 24 hours to complete, during which time the eater loses strength and the ability to resist damage. If not cured before the 24 hours end, the character dies and cannot be revived by any means.

4 Fungus colony possesses a bizarre hive mind and is able to communicate telepathically. The fungi know much about the dungeon, albeit expressed in odd, alien terms, and might convey this knowledge in return for services rendered. The referee is encouraged to make the services desired odd and nonsensical to the party in order to demonstrate this weird mind's needs and desires.

5 Fungus feeds off of magic. Each ten minutes spent in the area drains a random magical item of a charge/use, disenchants a potion, causes a caster to forget a spell, etc. Casting magic in the area results in a sudden spurt of fungus growth, which entangles the party, closes off exits, etc.

6 The fungus colony regularly walks through the dungeon's hallways, feeding off any stray organic matter it encounters. These jaunts might be slow creeps that grow over all in its path, or lemming-like surges as hordes of ambulatory toadstools knock down all who stand in its way.

7 Fungus exudes a sticky slime that covers it completely. Any adventurer coming into contact with the fungus risks becoming adhered to it. The more the adventurer struggles, the more entrapped he finds himself, until escape becomes impossible.

8 Fungus is harmless but possesses an unusual characteristic. Examples of these abnormalities include fungus that seems to sing or hum, sways as if blown by a breeze, grows in vaguely humanoid shapes, smells like fresh baked bread, or floats in the air on natural gas-filled sacks.

IS FOR GOLD

It is for gold that the brave or foolish venture into these unwelcoming subterranean locales. Without the prospect of gold, the party would pursue less fatal vocations. Gold is plentiful underground, either in the form of coins, ornamentation, or naturally occurring veins. It can never be accurately predicted where it may lie, however. Caches of forgotten gold are concealed in the most unlikely of places, thus encouraging the party to leave **No Stone Unturned**, no **Room** unsearched, and no **Door** left unopened. Without gold, there would be no adventure, so it should be in an abundant, perhaps never-ending, supply. Acquiring this plentiful substance, though, should never be easy. Unguarded gold, gleaming in the light of a torch, is always a prelude to danger.

TWENTY RANDOM FORMS OF GOLD

D20 Roll	
1	Gold object is in fact lead that's been coated with a gold-colored contact poison.
2	A cache of gold coins with strange engravings is found. When properly organized, the engravings form a map, a spell, an ancient prophecy, etc.
3	Coins are of a rare minting and worth 2-3 times their value to numismatists or sages.
4	Gold is in bullion form.
5	Gold is a worthless counterfeit.
6	1d10 of the gold coins are enchanted to automatically return to any owner who attunes them to his possession by sleeping with them under his pillow for five nights.
7	Objects that appear to be gold are really everyday ornaments covered in a rare form of deadly mold.
8	Gold is in the form of unstruck coin blanks. Possession of these blanks is illegal to anyone without royal permission. Characters face jail time if caught with them, but the local Thieves Guild will pay double for them.
9	Gold is enchanted to scream and cry when removed from its container.
10	A pile of gold serves as bait placed by an intelligent monster which lurks nearby, overhead, or otherwise concealed.
11	Gold coins are actually of a lesser variety (silver, copper, brass, etc.) that have been enameled. The coins still possess some value but not as much as originally believed.
12	Gold is in the form of ceremonial or decorative weapons and armor. They may be employed as combat gear but with very little effectiveness.
13	Gold bears a powerful curse. Those in possession of the gold might suffer penalties to rolls, encounter random monsters twice as often, grow suspicious of fellow adventurers, etc.
14	Adventurers discover the deed for a gold mine written out to the bearer. The adventurers must locate the mine, clear it of any hazards, and arrange mining and transport of the gold.
15	Party discovers a trail of gold coins leading off into the dungeon. These coins may lead to an ambush, be the result of a fellow adventurer's holed sack, or portend some even more nefarious event.
16	Gold emits strange subterranean radiations. Possessing more than two lbs. of this gold will cause the bearer to grow sick and die in 1d6 days unless the gold is discarded and curative magics are applied.
17	Gold coins have been "shaved" and only worth 1d4+5x10% normal value.
18	Bottles of rare gold ink are discovered. While worth 1d6x100 gold per bottle, this ink may also be used by wizards in enchanted writings.
19	Gold is in unprocessed form - nuggets, flakes, or dust.
20	Gold is in the form of gold thread which has been used to embroider a collection of ostentatious clothing.

IS ALSO FOR GUARDIANS

The dungeon is home to countless treasures that compel adventurers to risk their lives in hopes of plundering its subterranean riches. Most of these treasures are protected by either their rightful owners, cunning traps, or both. But some riches are entombed with the intent to be denied to everyone, laid away under the protection of fearsome guardians that take orders from no living being. These sentinels are no mere monsters, but terrible protectors possessing capabilities far beyond those of your average dungeon denizen, all to better perform their duties. Defeating these guardians with steel and sorcery is a risky gambit and typically the sentinel must be overcome with guile instead of brute or wizardly force.

Guardians come in all manner of forms: animated statues granted false life, extraplanar denizens bound into servitude, undead spectres oath-sworn to protect a valuable relic, and magically-constructed sentinels such as golems, automatons, and juggernauts are just a few examples of the guardians that might oppose plundering adventurers. Many serve long-dead masters, continuing to defend his or her riches after their corporeal remains have turned to dust, while others are specifically employed to deprive the forces of good or evil from a powerful artifact that could swing the balance of light and dark in the multiverse. Some guardians, like the treasures they defend, should be left alone.

TEN TERRIBLE GUARDIANS DEFENDING TERRIFIC TREASURES

D10   The guardian creature is...

1   An ephemeral nightmare that discerns the adventurers' worst fears and then assumes those forms, making it nearly impossible to attack with full strength. Prolonged battles with the guardian can drive one mad.

2   A sorcerous spider with webs strung throughout the world. Inflicting harm on the guardian causes the damage to be shared through its world-spanning webs. Any harm caused to the guardian is also inflicted on someone or something the attacker cares deeply about.

3   An oath-sworn living creature granted prolonged life by the sorceries that bind him to his duty. If defeated in battle, the magic causes the victor to become the new guardian, forced to defend the treasure until he too is defeated and the enchantment repeats again.

4   An animated construct that absorbs weapons and armor it comes in contact with, turning them against their former owners. The guardian becomes better protected as it incorporates stolen armor into its body and deals increased damage as it sprouts acquired blades from its fists and feet.

5   An incorporeal un-dead spirit that can take possession of living creatures. The guardian possesses one of the adventurers and turns him on his comrades, forcing them to fight one of their own. When that physical body is defeated, the guardian leaps into a new adventurer and the party must once again decide if killing their own is worth the riches the spirt protects.

6   An extraplanar creature that assumes the form of a legendary monster such as Cerebus, the Hydra, the tarasque, or similar mythical beast. The guardian draws its power from the collective myth of its assumed form, making it indestructible so long as there are those who believe in the legendary creature's existence. Only by piercing the guardian's disguise can the sentinel be defeated and the riches it guards claimed.

7   A creature from the Shadow Plane that lurks in the gloom, unseen by the party. It protects its charge by animating the adventurers' shadows and turning them against the PCs. The shadows can be defeated by plunging the area into darkness, but the Shadow Guardian's own power increases threefold when it is in the dark.

8   A clockwork construct capable of manipulating time. The guardian always strikes first, can rewind time to gain a second chance to avoid injury or successfully attack, and even pull additional copies of itself out of the time/space continuum to aid it against the adventurers.

9   An utterly alien thing from the Planes of Chaos that behaves in an illogical manner. Attacks and spells that cause injury make the guardian more formidable, while powers that heal or calm the creature inflict horrific wounds.

10   A shapeshifter that constantly assumes the forms of impervious creatures. It might transform into a lycanthrope, making it only vulnerable to silver, then change to a faerie creature struck only by cold iron, then shift into an un-dead beast harmed only by magic, and so forth. Unless the party has an arsenal of unusual weaponry or spells to combat it, the guardian will be almost impossible to kill.

AN A-TO-Z REFERENCE FOR CLASSIC DUNGEON DESIGN 25

IS FOR HALLWAYS

Like **Doors**, hallways are never to be trusted. Seemingly constructed of uniform stone blocks and of regular appearance, the hallway is never what is truly seems. Some slope almost undetected, guiding the party to deeper levels than they intended to venture into. Others hide **Traps**, concealed within, beneath, or above the unassuming stonework of the corridor. Still others **Echo** unsettlingly, announcing the presence of those who pass through them.

Even when of plain construction, hallways are very rarely clean and unadorned. When they are, it is a sure sign that a gelatinous cube dwells on this level and may soon pass this way again. More commonly, the hallways are strewn with reminders that the party is not the first to tread these corridors. Bloodstains, bones, burnt out torches, broken weapons, and pieces of shattered armor all lie scattered about the floor: tokens of the unlucky predecessors who came before them. Likewise the walls of hallways often sport adornments. Frescoes, mosaics, paintings, and bas-reliefs decorate the corridors and each may hide a sinister secret that awaits those who incautiously examine them.

TWENTY RANDOM DUNGEON HALLWAYS

1. The body of a massive creature — snake, purple worm, giant spider, bulette — clogs the hallway.

2. Hallway spins on a central pivot point, granting access or barring passage to other areas depending on its position.

3. The floor of the hallway is a mosaic of tiles that depicts geometric patterns or images of historic events.

4. Grates and vents line the floor and walls of the passageway. They might be for simple ventilation or a more sinister function.

5. The floor is upheaved, as if a giant creature burst from below, leaving a hole behind. This hole might be collapsed or lead to some deeper locale.

6. Broken weapons and bloodstains litter the floor, indicating a recent battle. No bodies are present, but blood trails lead off in at least two directions.

7. The corridor is immaculately clean. No dust, detritus, or debris mars the passageway and the floor and walls glisten as if recently scrubbed.

8. Two iron spikes have been driven into the ceiling here. Short pieces of old rope hang from them, but there is no indication of why they were placed here.

9. The ceiling of this corridor is cracked and drips with moisture that forms slimy puddles on the floor. Occasional cracks and groans issue from the weakened stone above.

10. The hallway is littered with fallen stonework and old skeletons. One skeleton seems to be pointing in a particular direction as determined by the referee.

11. A rusty signpost stands in the middle of an intersection.

12. The smoldering remains of a campfire and discarded ration wrappings sit in a dead-end corridor.

13. The hallway is choked with dust-laden webs, obscuring all vision.

14. Bas-reliefs along the walls depict an ancient and horrible religious ceremony, fearsome creatures, or other off-putting images.

15. Cairns of skulls and stones support tattered banners that mark the edges of a humanoid tribe's territory.

16. Glowing ceramic globes hang from chains down the length of the hallways, providing illumination and/or other surprises.

17. A rusty portcullis once barred passage down this corridor. The portcullis is no longer a barrier as its bars have been bent, sawed through, or rusted away.

18. The walls, floor, and ceiling of the corridor sport burn marks and soot, the stones cracked by some intense heat that ravaged the hall long ago.

19. Niches line the hallway, each holding the dusty bust of some long-forgotten individual who stares blindly ahead.

20. The walls of the hallway seep water, turning the floor slick with harmless mosses and fungi. Niter deposits encrust the stone walls.

IS ALSO FOR HAZARD

Dungeons dark and dank harbor myriad threats to life and limb: hungry monsters, terrible traps, and ancient sorcery all take a horrible toll on the adventurers who delve into the underworld. Not all these perils are intentional, however. Natural hazards and simple happenstance can also threaten the adventurers.

Hazards, unlike traps, are not the result of malicious planning or malignant intent, but natural or supernatural dangers that exist in the underworld environment of the dungeon. Hazards can range from crumbling stone that gives way when trod up to lingering aftereffects of a magical process to subterranean dangers like bad air or explosive mephitic gases. These hazards kill due to mere misfortune and not evil design, but that's of little consolation to the adventurers slain by dungeon hazards.

A HALF-SCORE OF HAZARDOUS HAPPENINGS

D12   The hazard encountered is...

1   Subterranean water has eroded the stone beneath the floor of a room or hallway, leaving a cavity under the flagstones. Stepping on the eroded space causes the floor to give way, dropping the unfortunate into a water-slick tunnel that leads deeper into the dungeon or ends abruptly on jagged rocks.

2   The air in this location is bad, poisoned by subterranean gases. Adventurers entering into this air pocket must make saving throws to avoid passing out and asphyxiating. Alternately, the bad air might be explosive and the party risks detonating the hazardous gases with their torches and lanterns.

3   Mud covers a stretch of dungeon corridor or chamber, seemingly a product of natural erosion and weakened earth. The mud is in truth a patch of quicksand capable of dragging anyone entering the liquid earth to a drowning death.

4   An asphalt lake stretches out before the adventurers, a product of a petroleum seep at the lake's heart. The viscous raw petroleum is sticky and unrelenting, imprisoning anyone who falls into it. The substance is also extremely flammable and an errant spark can turn the entire reservoir into a hellish conflagration capable of burning the party to ashes.

5   The ceiling in this region is lined with "snotties," single-celled bacteria that resemble soft stalactites. Snotties are naturally acidic, dripping caustic slime down onto anything that passes, eating away at flesh, metal, and leather in moments. The adventurers might not realize the "stalactites" are something else until they begin to burn.

6   The area is home to a vein of eldritch ore that reacts violently when in the presence of permanent magical enchantments. The ore is difficult to detect visually, but whenever a non-consumable magical item is brought near the mineral, lightning erupts from the object, cascading about to strike other enchanted objects and electrifying their owners.

7   A particularly foul section of dungeon (midden, latrine, butcher's shambles, etc.) is home to disease-carrying bacteria, vermin, or other infectious vector. Adventurers searching through the area must make saving throws to avoid contracting the disease. The infection can range from mildly incapacitating to swiftly lethal and only magical or herbal healing can stop the infection.

8   The dungeon is located in a flood zone and is normally (relatively) dry and safe. However, when thunderstorms break in the mountains above the dungeon, swift-flowing torrents breach the dungeon, drowning and crushing its occupants. PCs exploring the dungeon when the storm hits must move fast to avoid dying in the flooded dungeon.

9   A naturally occurring breach between planes exists in the dungeon, periodically infecting the undercroft with energies native to that plane of existence. The dungeon may occasionally erupt in flames, be filled with howling winds, become lethally cold, or even drain the very life force from those within the underworld. The breach may be closed permanently, but will require powerful magic.

10   A deposit of highly magnetized lodestone is adjacent to part of the dungeon, exerting intense magnetic attraction on ferrous metals passing through the area. Metal weapons and armor are yanked against the wall/floor/ceiling closest to the deposit, possibly taking their owners with them. The magnetic attraction is so strong that only exceptional strength can tear the items free, possibly forcing the party to turn back or to venture forth lacking their best weapons and armor.

11   Mephitic gases birthed in the chthonic realm permeate this part of the dungeon. The gases cause confusion and hallucinations in any surface creature breathing them. PCs failing their saving throws may flee in terror from the hallucinations they experience, wander off to be eaten alone, or turn on their friends, believing them to be horrible monsters.

12   Subterranean bacteria infects unpreserved foodstuffs, either turning the food inedible (and possibly poisonous) or destroying it outright. Unless the party has access to magic that can purify the tainted rations, they will suffer exhaustion and its side effects if they persist exploring the dungeon. Finally, a reason to buy iron rations over normal rations—and to memorize *purify food and water*!

IS FOR INSCRIPTIONS

Those who have come before you have left writings to mark their passage. Cryptic clues, warnings written in blood, ancient riddles, strange sigils, and curious runes are found inscribed on surfaces deep beneath the earth. Some provide hints as to where treasures may be found, while others seek to keep the party from venturing further into the dungeon. Some inscriptions are easily deciphered, having been written in the language of the surface races. Others are more arcane, requiring useful spells, cipher wheels, or the knowledge of dead languages to decode.

Inscriptions can be deadly to read or to speak aloud. One never knows if some strange writing is actually a *symbol*, a *glyph of warding*, or *explosive runes*. Or perhaps those writings are words of power that, if spoken, let slip the chains imprisoning an ancient and eldritch evil, turning it loose once again on the world. As with most things in the dungeon, even the writings on the walls sometimes conceal hidden dangers.

EIGHT INTERESTING INSCRIPTIONS

D8 Roll	
1	Wall bears the last will and testament of a dead adventurer leaving all his earthly possessions to whomever finds this message. In order to claim their inheritance though, the party must return this inscription intact to a major city or town. This could prove difficult.

2 A formula for a new spell written by a deranged wizard. If deciphered correctly, a new spell may be learned by a spell-caster. Due to the wizard's insanity, there is a 66% chance that the spell will actually be dangerous to the caster the first time it is attempted. The exact effects are left to the referee but damage taken, undesired shape change, turning to stone, and the like are suggested outcomes.

3 Crude graffiti written in a humanoid tongue and directed at another species or clan. It may be memorized phonetically even if the language it is written in is not understood. This could have effects leading from the humorous, if used in the presence of those of same race as the original writer's, to the disastrous, such as if used amongst those whom the vulgarities are directed at.

4 Helpful directions written in a common tongue. These directions could warn of an upcoming trap, point the way to the nearest exit, or provide clues to a hidden treasure. There is a 20% chance that these directions are actually intended to lure adventurers into danger, rather than help.

5 Glowing glyphs mark the walls here. If touched in the proper order (determined by the referee), a concealed chamber, staircase, or other feature is revealed. If pressed in incorrect order, a trap might be triggered.

6 Scrawled on a wall by a dead man's hand is a name. Unbeknownst to the party, it is the true name of a powerful entity: devil or demon, powerful mage, high priest, etc. who will go to any extreme to keep that secret name safe.

7 A cryptic word scribbled in the pages of an ordinary book works as a password, command word, or incantation in another part of the dungeon.

8 Adventurers discover an obelisk similar to the Rosetta Stone. With a month of uninterrupted study, one could learn a lost or rare tongue such as the language of birds, a long dead race, the speech of the heavens, or similar forms of communication.

J IS FOR JEWELS

Like **Gold**, jewels are what drive expeditions into the dangerous places beneath the earth. Less common than gold, but more valuable and more easily transportable, jewels are desired by most races, but some value them higher than most. A gnome casts his eye upon a well-cut gem the way a dwarf covets his gold.

Jewels take many forms in the dungeon. They are found loose amongst hoards, adorning weapons, crafted into the covers of **Books**, or embedded in curious **Statues**. They come in a rainbow of colors; a seasoned adventurer will soon learn to discern the most valuable ones amongst the dross, but even experience may fail a hearty dungeon-delving soul. Many jewels are more valuable than they first appear, being either cut by a skilled jeweler or possessing mystic powers not visible to the naked eye. Some jewels have been known to explode, are protected by things not of this world, trap the very souls of those who handle them, or exact a horrible price on those guilty of their theft.

A DOZEN UNUSUAL PROPERTIES FOR JEWELS

D12 Roll	
1	The gem is of unusual hue or clarity for its type and is worth up to 5 times its normal value.
2	The gem is carved into a decorative shape — flower, heart, star, etc. Because of the workmanship, the gem is worth 2-4 times its usual value and may possess other properties.
3	The stone is enchanted and serves as a repository for a single spell. If the stone is smashed or damaged, the spell takes effect centered around the gem but with otherwise normal effect.
4	A necklace adorned with 1d8 amber stones is found. Encased in each stone is a strange insectile form. These may be merely natural byproducts of the amber's formation or they may have supernatural properties if freed from the stones.
5	Gem is of unusual origin such as a toadstone, a trichobezoar from a medusa, or the hardened ambergris of the Leviathan.
6	Jewel provides additional protection against poisons, disease, insanity, spells, etc. when worn against the skin.
7	Jewel is part of a legendary collection — the Crown Jewels, the Seven Stones of the Maharajah, the Crimson Star Stones, etc. — and is recognized by jewelers or lapidaries. The jewel is one that has been stolen and possession of it may result in the authorities attempting to reclaim it and arrest the adventurers for its theft.
8	The gemstone is horribly flawed and only worth half its normal value.
9	Jewel reveals hidden properties of objects when they are viewed through the stone. Suggested detected properties include object's general health, true form, magical auras, presence of poison, veracity of statements, etc.
10	Jewel attracts creatures of a certain type (giant insects, ghosts, cats, snakes, etc.) that could prove distracting or dangerous to its owner.
11	Jewel is of a type used in magic spells or rituals and is of exquisite quality. Using this stone in the rite increases the chance of success, ensures maximum results, or otherwise improves the outcome of the spell.
12	Jewel is actually the egg of some unknown creature. If left in the possession of a warm-blooded creature for a period determined by the referee, the jewel hatches. The results of such an event are left to the referee to decide and could be either beneficial or harmful to the jewel's possessor.

IS FOR KOBOLDS

Despite the inclusion of "Dragons" in the title of the game, there is perhaps no monster more often encountered by adventuring parties than the lowly kobold. Short, scaly, dog-like creatures, kobolds are not related to dragons in any way. To think as much would be absurd. The sounds of their yipping voices indicate that the party's first test by combat is at hand. Whether the kobolds are mere annoyances or "Tuckerized," kobold blood has wetted the swords of more 1st level adventurers than any other monster, earning their place amongst the tropes of *Dungeons & Dragons*.

While the table below is intended to make any tribe of kobolds a more memorable encounter, these permutations could be applied to any group of small humanoid monsters with similar results.

TEN UNIQUE KOBOLD TRIBES

D10 Roll	
1	The kobolds have bred rats of abnormal size, which they ride into battle like goblins do worgs. Smaller rats might be employed as bloodhounds or as packs of "war rats" led by a whip-wielding handler.
2	Kobolds follow a strict warrior code similar to bushido or chivalry.
3	These kobolds have discovered an incendiary or explosive concoction of minerals and fungus. The kobolds hurl grenade-like containers of this mixture at enemies, as well as using it in booby traps. It could even be used as a volatile form of gunpowder…
4	Kobolds adorn themselves with war paint they believe protects them in battle. The referee is left to determine if this paint has any actual in-game effect.
5	Some kobolds are master craftsmen in one field. Any object they have made from that field is of increased value or function. Examples include pottery as strong as iron, rope that supports twice its normal capacity, herbal cures with almost magic results, etc.
6	The kobolds survive as service personnel for the dungeon. They relay messages, perform custodial duties, repair and reset traps, and maintain the dungeon for the stronger monsters. They might even be hired by the adventurers as guides, torch bearers, or porters.
7	Through fortifications and superior numbers, the kobolds have established a monopoly on some vital resource — fungus gardens, fresh water, etc. The kobolds grow rich and well-supplied by selling and trading this resource to other intelligent dungeon creatures.
8	The kobolds have discovered a cache of potent weapons and armor — fine dwarven steel, enchanted dark elf weapons, etc. — which makes them much more formidable than the average kobold tribe.
9	The kobolds, through exposure to strange subterranean radiation, have undergone bizarre mutations. These kobolds now possess such strange traits as abnormal size, two heads, the ability to crawl on walls and ceilings like spiders, grow quills they can throw like porcupines, etc. A memorable tribe indeed!
10	The kobolds worship an ancient neo-otyugh that dwells in a local midden/cesspit as a god. They scavenge garbage, rotting food, corpses, and the like as offerings for the "Trash God." They might decide a weak party would make a fine offering.

IS FOR LEVERS

Protruding from floors and walls, these mechanical devices are often the cause of many arguments amongst adventurers. Pull it or don't pull it? These debates usually last until a monster is drawn to their location by the intense bickering or a brave or foolish soul throws the lever to the dismay of the others. In either case, the results are rarely uninteresting.

Levers are the litmus test to determine how courageous or brash a party is, especially if there are no hints to the possible consequences of throwing that lever. Once thrown, an array of results may confront the party. Hidden passages are revealed, monsters are unleashed, traps are sprung, ability scores rise or fall, electricity arcs across the chamber, whole **Rooms** descend, **Statues** come to life, or simply that nothing observable occurs are all common results of a thrown lever. When stuck for ideas, a referee need do nothing more than place a lever in the center of a barren room and wait for the party to work themselves into a frenzy.

THIRTY RESULTS FOR A PULLED LEVER

1	Drops gates/portcullises throughout the dungeon level.		16	Causes a useful item to be dispensed.
2	Triggers alarm — monsters come to investigate.		17	Hidden door opens.
3	Gout of fire envelopes the lever-puller.		18	Activates/deactivates trap in another location.
4	Floods room with water.		19	Puller ages 1d20 years.
5	Causes liquids in the room to boil.		20	Whirling vortex carries puller off to some other location.
6	Frees dangerous monsters to prowl the dungeon.		21	Triggers trap in the room.
7	Summons enchanted servant to do the puller's biding.		22	Saps the spirit of the puller, resulting in loss of 1 random ability point.
8	Infuses puller with spiritual energy. Puller gains 1 random ability point.		23	Activates anti-magic field temporarily neutralizing any spells or magic items in the room.
9	Causes room to descend/ascend.		24	Activates powerful magnets. Armor-clad adventurers incapacitated.
10	Trapdoor opens under party.		25	Nothing happens.
11	Activates self-destruct sequence.		26	A magical banquet, complete with table and chairs, appears.
12	Magically cleans and refreshes the puller.		27	Erases the puller's memory of the last 24 hours.
13	Concealed ceiling vents open and begin to rain snakes, toads, vermin, etc. on the party.		28	Illusionary music begins to play within the room.
14	Causes torches, candles, fireplace, etc. in the room to ignite.		29	Alters temperature of the room (sweltering heat or frigid cold).
15	Locks/unlocks doors within the dungeon.		30	One-armed Bandit — pulling this lever randomly increases/decreases the puller's personal money as determined by the referee.

IS ALSO FOR LEVELS

Adventurers use the term "dungeon" to refer to any subterranean complex housing monsters and treasure. Some are small, compact places, easily explored in a day. But any veteran adventurer knowns that a true dungeon is a massive place containing layer upon layer of chambers and the means to access them. Each of these levels of the dungeon houses terrifying residents and vast treasures waiting to be plundered.

Most of these dungeon levels are connected by **Stairs** or similar mundane means of access. But, in the bizarre subterranean world, these ordinary methods are not the only way to travel from dungeon level to dungeon level. A carelessly pulled **Lever** might send the party hurtling down a chute to arrive in a monster's den on the next lowest level! Even stranger connectors are said to exist by experienced dungeon explorers.

Once the new level is reached, the party has entered terra incognito once again. Most levels are hewn from the surrounding stone or are comprised of **Caves**. Humanoid races, vermin, and weird underground creatures dwell there. But other levels are built with far less prosaic functions or inhabitants in mind. These levels house the greatest dangers... but also the greatest treasures.

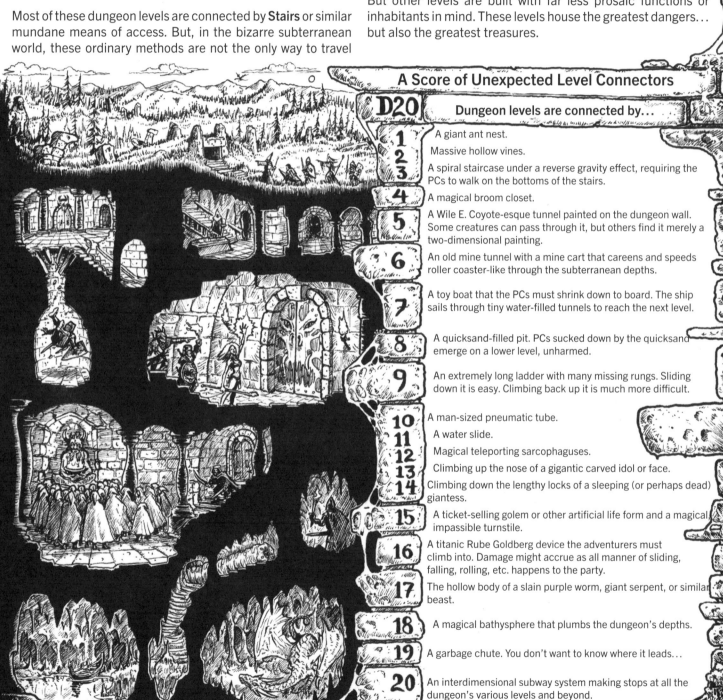

A Score of Unexpected Level Connectors

D20	Dungeon levels are connected by...
1	A giant ant nest.
2	Massive hollow vines.
3	A spiral staircase under a reverse gravity effect, requiring the PCs to walk on the bottoms of the stairs.
4	A magical broom closet.
5	A Wile E. Coyote-esque tunnel painted on the dungeon wall. Some creatures can pass through it, but others find it merely a two-dimensional painting.
6	An old mine tunnel with a mine cart that careens and speeds roller coaster-like through the subterranean depths.
7	A toy boat that the PCs must shrink down to board. The ship sails through tiny water-filled tunnels to reach the next level.
8	A quicksand-filled pit. PCs sucked down by the quicksand emerge on a lower level, unharmed.
9	An extremely long ladder with many missing rungs. Sliding down it is easy. Climbing back up it is much more difficult.
10	A man-sized pneumatic tube.
11	A water slide.
12	Magical teleporting sarcophaguses.
13	Climbing up the nose of a gigantic carved idol or face.
14	Climbing down the lengthy locks of a sleeping (or perhaps dead) giantess.
15	A ticket-selling golem or other artificial life form and a magical, impassible turnstile.
16	A titanic Rube Goldberg device the adventurers must climb into. Damage might accrue as all manner of sliding, falling, rolling, etc. happens to the party.
17	The hollow body of a slain purple worm, giant serpent, or similar beast.
18	A magical bathysphere that plumbs the dungeon's depths.
19	A garbage chute. You don't want to know where it leads...
20	An interdimensional subway system making stops at all the dungeon's various levels and beyond.

William McAusland

TWENTY DUNGEON LEVEL THEMES

D20 Roll	The dungeon level is…
1	The workshop of a mad scientist or crazed mage. It is filled with terrible machines and animated constructs such as golems or robots.
2	A goblin temple dedicated to a forgotten god. The goblins wear outrageous costumes and engage in curious rites such as spider wrestling and monkey dances.
3	The secret meeting hall of the region's dragons. They attend these meetings polymorphed to fit into the smaller rooms and halls, and only reveal their true shapes if attacked.
4	The resting place of some terrible, gigantic monster (a kaiju-sized creature, a gargantuan dragon, a violent titan, etc.). It is kept in magical stasis by wards or devout priests. If those are rendered incapable of performing their duty, catastrophe ensues.
5	A contingency hideout for a powerful thief. Filled with traps and his most trusted henchmen, the hideout is an already dangerous place. Then, the master thief arrives, fleeing other trouble…
6	An intricately crafted dwarven music hall filled with chambers that resonate with sound when stringed instruments are played.
7	A connector between planes of existence. Extraplanar creatures come and go through it on their way to other dimensions. Perhaps rival planes, such as water and fire, mix at the level's center to create unusual dimensional conditions?
8	The birthing grounds of ALL the world's kobolds.
9	The repository for all living creatures'—or perhaps just one species'—"soul candles." Each creature has a single divinely-created candle that burns for the duration of their lifetime. When the candle is extinguished, the creature dies. The gods store them here under immense protection.
10	A storage place for improperly-manufactured or cursed magical items. The level appears rich with magic wands, swords, potions, and other enchanted object, but none work as intended.
11	In the shape of a vast sailing ship. It's possible the dungeon was created as the tomb of a Viking-like jarl or maybe the level itself is capable of sailing the Astral Realm when certain controls are operated.
12	Entirely out of phase. Explorers can pass through its halls and corridors, but all the dungeon's contents—including the mounds of treasure that fill its ghostly chambers—cannot be touched. A potion, ointment, or gateway somewhere on the level allows the PCs to shift out of phase and interact with the dungeon proper.
13	An embassy between the subterranean world and the surface realm. Operated by a neutral race capable of visiting both regions with minimum difficulty, the level contains meeting rooms, a bazaar, and a plethora of shady characters and hidden enemies.
14	Built to get increasing smaller in size the further one travels. Rooms and halls are initially constructed for man-sized creatures or larger, but by the time the furthest chambers are reached, even small creatures must stoop or crawl. Monsters inhabiting the rooms are sized accordingly.
15	A place where life and death is reversed. Attacks and damage-dealing spells restore health to their targets, while curative magic inflicts harm upon the supposed beneficiaries of the spell's energy. This could be the side-effect of an ancient spell or a weird natural phenomenon.
16	Alive. It reacts to the adventurers' presence like a body reacts to an invading virus. Alien "antibody" defenders are dispatched and the very walls, floors, and ceilings respond to being probed, marked, or attacked.
17	On fire. Normally, this level is an average dungeon level, but a catastrophe struck just before the adventurers arrived and it is now burning. For extra tension, the means the adventurers used to reach the level collapse or burn behind them, potentially trapping them here unless an alternate escape route is found.
18	Filled with weird mephitic gases that affect living creatures. Those breathing the gases might turn gaseous themselves, gain new powers, lose other powers, or otherwise be transformed. The level is filled with undead or constructed creatures that are immune to the gases' effects, or home to subterranean creatures who use the gases' power to their advantage!
19	A wildlife preserve for endangered dungeon creatures such as the pink ooze, the rot monster (whose antenna turn cloth to tatters), and the giant subterranean dodo. Needless to say, the preserve's caretakers will not be happy if the PCs slaughter these rare creatures!
20	A self-destruct mechanism. The level is rigged to explode, collapse, or otherwise catastrophically fail, taking all the levels above with it. This is accomplished by levers, magical symbols, breaking seals, or similar processes. The self-destruct sequence is difficult, but not impossible to activate, especially when curious and incautious adventurers are concerned!

IS FOR MAGIC

Like **Gold** and **Jewels**, magic draws the adventurers to plumb the unknown depth of the dungeon. Risking life and limb to lay their hands on everything from the legendary sword of a past ruler to a cool blue bottle that holds a *potion of healing*, magical items are a potent lure for greedy adventurers. And, like an addiction, magical items only encourage the cycle of dungeon delving. With access to more potent magical devices, the adventurers push deeper into the shadowy halls in search of even more powerful magical rewards.

But not all magic in the dungeon comes in easily transportable forms. Weird spells and arcane effects linger in the dark, subjecting adventuring parties to perils unseen at the hands of living wizards. The days of yore contain many secrets, some of which linger long after their creators have passed on. An **Altar** or **Statue** may impose strange effects upon those unwary to touch them: swapping identities or alignments, laying down curses, or causing the very magic the party normally relies upon to act randomly and dangerously. Golems, enchanted statues, animated furniture, and fearsome Things created in arcane laboratories wander the dusty corridors that wind under the feet of more sensible folks, awaiting the coming of visitors from above. Shimmering portals hang in the air, providing egress to places unknown, providing a handy escape route for an endangered band of adventurers willing to take the plunge.

3d20 Roll		3d20 Roll	
3	An archway that swaps the personalities of those who walk through it.	32	A bath that cures disease or poison.
4	A chamber pot that sends small bits of non-living matter to another plane.	33	A harpsichord/pipe organ that plays magical sheet music producing spell-like effects.
5	A mirror that transforms the face of whoever looks into it.	34	A magical mouth that appears bearing grim warnings.
6	A pantry that keeps food stored within it permanently fresh and edible.	35	A wardrobe that mends clothing and armor placed inside it.
7	An enchanted clockwork bird in a gilded cage.	36	A hopping coffin/sarcophagus that wanders the dungeon.
8	A levitating egg-shaped stone covered in strange symbols.	37	A talking stag's head mounted on a plaque above a fireplace.
9	A throne that allows any who sit upon it to view distant sections of the dungeon.	38	A cursed bookmark/paperweight that eats ink.
10	A cistern that magically refills itself at sunrise.	39	A spinning wheel that turns wool into gold (or vice versa).
11	A staircase that leads to another plane of existence.	40	A forge that never needs fuel or grows cold.
12	A peppermill that grinds gemstones into miniature servants.	41	A bed that provides restful sleep in half the usual time.
13	A window that looks out onto a peaceful, sunlit garden, despite its location deep underground.	42	An animated picture, tapestry, or mural.
14	A reflecting pool filled with miniature ships which reenact famous sea battles.	43	A never-emptying cask of wine or keg of ale.
15	Crockery that produces bland but nourishing food once each day.	44	A bearskin rug that attacks intruders.
16	An hourglass that pauses or speeds up time for one minute.	45	An inkpot the produces magical (invisible, encrypted, auto-translating, etc.) ink.
17	A levitating chandelier that lowers and rises on command.	46	A wind-up minstrel that plays the lute and sings.
19	A child-size horse and chariot that moves on command.	47	A fountain of living purple flame.
19	An animated cloak stand that follows anyone wearing a cloak until they remove it and hang it on the stand.	48	A holy/unholy water font that doubles as a scrying pool.
20	Gaming tiles (dominos, mahjong, etc.) that perform divinations.	49	Enchanted candies that allow the eater to "sweet talk" others into doing what he wishes.
21	A Wheel of Fortune that bestows boons or banes upon the spinner.	50	An alcove that teleports any who enter to a hidden chamber or dungeon sub-level.
22	A monocle that reveals secret doors.	51	A rock tumbler that increases the value of gems or transforms normal stones into magical sling projectiles.
23	An animal mask that turns the wearer into the animal depicted.	52	A blackboard that answers questions written upon it with sage-like accuracy.
24	A water pipe that produces visions of the future when smoked.	53	A painted diagram of the dungeon that shows the location of any member of the adventuring band when commanded.
25	An enchanted ceiling that duplicates the night sky and the movement of heavenly bodies in it.	54	A doormat that teleports anyone standing on it to the other side of any closed door it is placed in front of.
26	A doorframe that garbles books and scrolls that pass through it.	55	A set of bagpipes that produces clouds of fog, smoke, bubbles, or other gaseous substance.
27	A pair of braziers that walk on their short iron legs, accompanying he who commands them.	56	An enchanted blanket that doubles the normal natural healing time of anyone wrapped in it.
28	A pillar or column that rises and falls on command, serving as an elevator to reach overhead areas.	57	A whetstone that temporarily enchants any bladed weapon.
29	An ordinary looking container that holds an imprisoned extra-dimensional being of great power.	58	A dumbwaiter that ascends to a secure extra-dimensional space.
30	A talking skeleton imprisoned in solid rock.	59	A patrolling elemental comprised of refuse and dungeon debris.
31	A pair of shackles that cancel any magical ability of whoever is restrained by them.	60	The statuette of a pig that oinks when brought within 10' of poison.

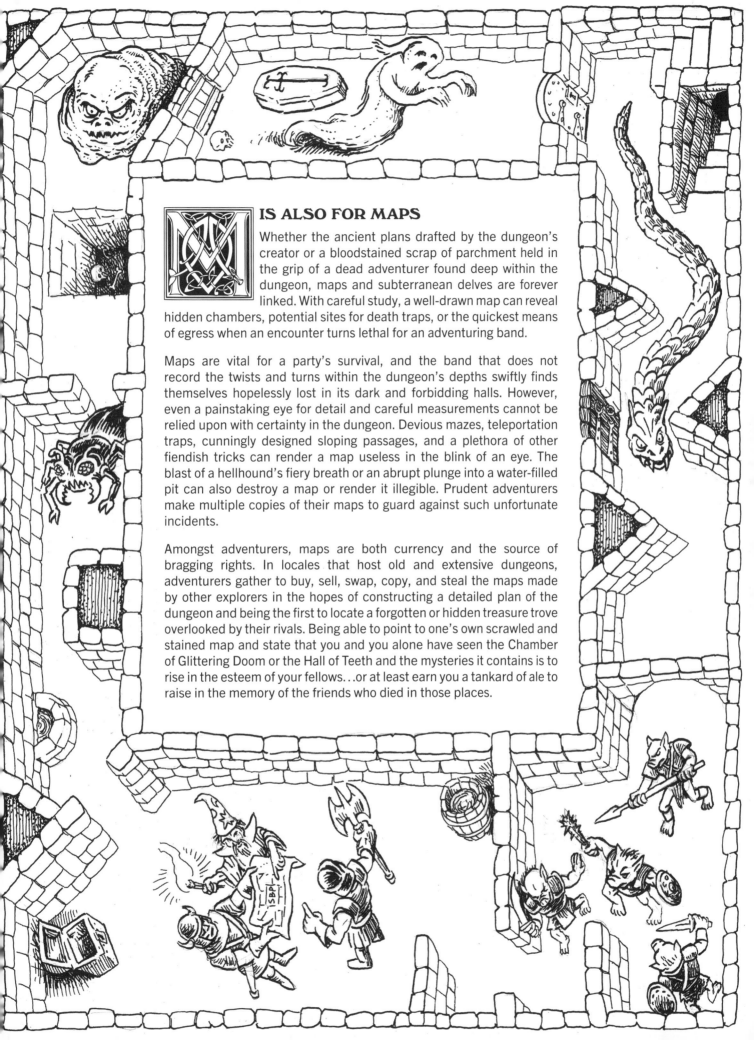

IS ALSO FOR MAPS

Whether the ancient plans drafted by the dungeon's creator or a bloodstained scrap of parchment held in the grip of a dead adventurer found deep within the dungeon, maps and subterranean delves are forever linked. With careful study, a well-drawn map can reveal hidden chambers, potential sites for death traps, or the quickest means of egress when an encounter turns lethal for an adventuring band.

Maps are vital for a party's survival, and the band that does not record the twists and turns within the dungeon's depths swiftly finds themselves hopelessly lost in its dark and forbidding halls. However, even a painstaking eye for detail and careful measurements cannot be relied upon with certainty in the dungeon. Devious mazes, teleportation traps, cunningly designed sloping passages, and a plethora of other fiendish tricks can render a map useless in the blink of an eye. The blast of a hellhound's fiery breath or an abrupt plunge into a water-filled pit can also destroy a map or render it illegible. Prudent adventurers make multiple copies of their maps to guard against such unfortunate incidents.

Amongst adventurers, maps are both currency and the source of bragging rights. In locales that host old and extensive dungeons, adventurers gather to buy, sell, swap, copy, and steal the maps made by other explorers in the hopes of constructing a detailed plan of the dungeon and being the first to locate a forgotten or hidden treasure trove overlooked by their rivals. Being able to point to one's own scrawled and stained map and state that you and you alone have seen the Chamber of Glittering Doom or the Hall of Teeth and the mysteries it contains is to rise in the esteem of your fellows…or at least earn you a tankard of ale to raise in the memory of the friends who died in those places.

TWELVE UNUSUAL MAPS FOUND IN THE DUNGEON

D12   The map...

1   Is sentient and can answer questions regarding the different chambers depicted on it. Perhaps the map is inhabited by the spirit of a slain adventurer or was drafted by a magical architect hired to create traps within the delve. Its veracity is by no means beyond reproach nor is the tongue it speaks necessarily one still in common usage.

2   Was drafted by an entity not entirely of this plane. Being drawn by a creature who could perceive more than three dimensions, the map is alien and incomprehensible until viewed from the Astral, Ethereal, or other plane of existence. Only then do the strange squiggles and symbols on the map make sense to mundane eyes.

3   Is animated and attempts to crawl away when not secured. The map once resided in a special repository deep in the dungeon and was ensorcelled to return to its proper resting place when not held by authorized parties. There is a way to keep the map in one's possession, but to do so the holder must convince the map he is authorized to own it. The method of proving this authorization can be dangerous, humiliating, or simply a matter of producing the appropriate credentials.

4   Is largely blank except for a few uninteresting chambers, leaving plenty of space for the party's mapper to add more to it. Unfortunately, the map's parchment is cursed and the plan is subtly altered each time the map is put away. A door on the map might vanish or a corridor might be redrawn with an incorrect bend or length. Unless a copy of the map is made, the party is unlikely to notice the changes until it is too late.

5   Is in liquid form. Contained in a plain glass bottle, this odd liquid must be sipped to gain the benefits of the map. Each time a small amount of liquid is consumed, the drinker receives an accurate mental picture of the dungeon (or simply his immediate surroundings). This cerebral image is fleeting, lasting no more than a minute or so before fading from the drinker's mind. In order to make longer use of the liquid map, he must either quickly sketch a copy (and perhaps make errors in his haste) or sample from the bottle regularly and risk running out of the cartographical fluid at a crucial moment.

6   Is visible only under specific conditions. While a map with symbols that reveal themselves in moonlight is a fantasy staple, that is but one example. Others include an oilskin map that shows its chambers when immersed in liquid or a plan sketched on gauzy material that must be exposed to warm breezes to read correctly. Maps drawn by evil cults could be legible when steeped in the blood of a living sacrifice, only then revealing secret places best unvisited by goodly folk.

7   Is drawn in a most inhospitable place. An ancient dwarven map might now be found scrawled on the throat of an active volcano. A valuable floor plan might be inscribed on the actual floor of a dangerous monster's den. Perhaps the map the party seeks was in the possession of an explorer who met his end in the belly of a great beast, and his last act in life was to draw the plan on the stomach walls of the creature that ate him.

8   Is a temporal anomaly. Seemingly a normal dungeon plan, following the map leads the party backwards or forwards in time, allowing them to visit parts of the dungeon when they were new or in the final stages of collapse. Unexpected denizens are encountered in rooms existing before or after the party's current epoch, and woe unto the party who loses their map when outside their own time period.

9   Is seemingly a master plan of the dungeon's traps and the locations of the means to disarm them. Experiments to prove the map's authenticity seem to support its veracity but unwittingly set in motion more calamitous events. As each switch is thrown to disarm a trap (real or imagined), hidden machinery or spells are made active, culminating in a death trap of extreme lethality or the unleashing of a creature best left bound.

10   Is a dungeon unto itself. When examined, it shares no similarities to the dungeon the party is currently exploring, but if the proper steps are taken, the party can enter the map itself and visit a completely unknown adventuring site. In order to enter this two-dimensional dungeon, the party needs to sketch themselves onto the map, with the artistic skill of the drawing hand determining their appearance and capabilities once inside the drawn delve. Imagine the frustrations of a poorly rendered party who must overcome fearsome monsters with stick-figure weapons and armor!

11   Is capable of altering the dungeon itself. Drawn on an unusual material (human skin, dinosaur hide, angel feathers, etc.), the map is linked to the dungeon and any changes made to the map are reflected in the delve's layout. New passageways sketched onto the map suddenly appear, travel distances are reduced by folding the map upon itself, and doorways vanish with the stroke of an inked quill. These changes might be permanent or temporary, and the map itself may only allow a finite number of alterations before losing its power.

12   Has no right to exist. The plan details a place that has no worldly counterpart. It could be a map to a place one of the PCs regularly visits in dreams or be the floor plan to the stronghold he one day intends to build. There is no reasonable explanation to the map's existence, but there is a cartographer's name sketched on the edge of the plan. Adventurers must seek out the mysterious mapper to discover how he created this inexplicable plan.

IS FOR NO STONE LEFT UNTURNED

Despite the limitless supply of **Gold**, **Jewels**, and **Magic** in the dungeon, the party knows that if this bounty was easily found, someone would have carried it away long ago. As such, whatever treasure remains must be well-secreted in some unassuming place. To uncover this theoretical hoard, no square inch of the dungeon must be left undisturbed. Walls must be searched for secret doors, furniture dismantled to uncover hidden compartments, chests upturned and painstakingly measured to reveal false bottoms, **Levers** must be thrown, **Statues** moved, teeth examined for fillings of precious metal, and prisoners interrogated to reveal what they know.

These determined efforts may be rewarded, but the risk often outweighs the gain. The time required to unearth every secret the dungeon conceals only provides more opportunities for wandering denizens to chance upon the preoccupied adventurers. Encouraging the party to be thorough must be tempered by the tendency for overzealous searches to turn a dungeon crawl into an archeological survey of the site. It is perfectly acceptable for a party to miss a secret cache of wealth, especially if the dungeon is a reoccurring location in the campaign. What the party misses the first time may be discovered on the second, third, or thirtieth trip into its depths.

TWENTY RANDOM PLACES TO HIDE THINGS

D20 Roll	Hidden In/By
1	Under a loose flagstone
2	In a hollowed-out book
3	Over a door
4	Invisible
5	False bottom of chest
6	Inside a large urn/jar/amphora
7	Secret compartment under a stair step
8	Behind a painting/tapestry/other wall-hanging
9	Inside a cheap statuette
10	Camouflaged/concealed by illusion
11	Underside of a table/desk
12	In a hollowed-out chair/table leg
13	In an old pair of boots
14	Extra-dimensional space inside a mirror or painting
15	Inside a fireplace — hidden under the ashes, stashed in the chimney, etc.
16	Underneath a mattress
17	Amongst normal items of the same type — books in a bookcase, cloak in a wardrobe, etc.
18	Behind a large piece of furniture — bookshelves, bed, desk, divan, etc.
19	Underneath a floor covering — rug, hay, dirt, leaf litter
20	Secret wall compartment

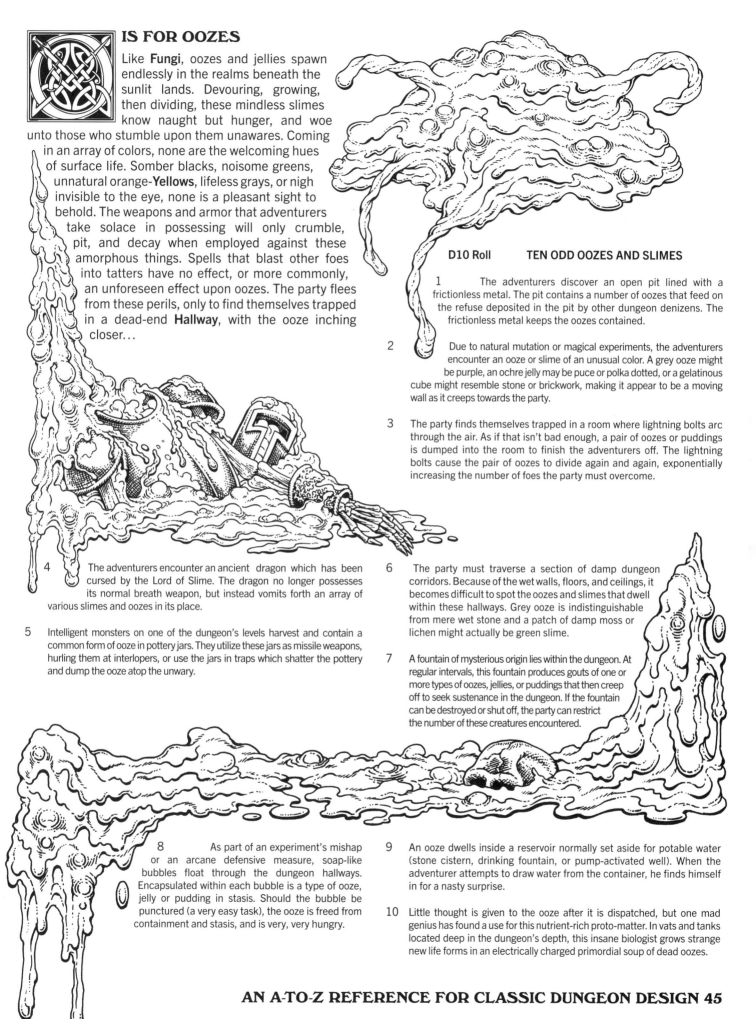

IS FOR OOZES

Like **Fungi**, oozes and jellies spawn endlessly in the realms beneath the sunlit lands. Devouring, growing, then dividing, these mindless slimes know naught but hunger, and woe unto those who stumble upon them unawares. Coming in an array of colors, none are the welcoming hues of surface life. Somber blacks, noisome greens, unnatural orange-**Yellows**, lifeless grays, or nigh invisible to the eye, none is a pleasant sight to behold. The weapons and armor that adventurers take solace in possessing will only crumble, pit, and decay when employed against these amorphous things. Spells that blast other foes into tatters have no effect, or more commonly, an unforeseen effect upon oozes. The party flees from these perils, only to find themselves trapped in a dead-end **Hallway**, with the ooze inching closer…

D10 Roll   TEN ODD OOZES AND SLIMES

1   The adventurers discover an open pit lined with a frictionless metal. The pit contains a number of oozes that feed on the refuse deposited in the pit by other dungeon denizens. The frictionless metal keeps the oozes contained.

2   Due to natural mutation or magical experiments, the adventurers encounter an ooze or slime of an unusual color. A grey ooze might be purple, an ochre jelly may be puce or polka dotted, or a gelatinous cube might resemble stone or brickwork, making it appear to be a moving wall as it creeps towards the party.

3   The party finds themselves trapped in a room where lightning bolts arc through the air. As if that isn't bad enough, a pair of oozes or puddings is dumped into the room to finish the adventurers off. The lightning bolts cause the pair of oozes to divide again and again, exponentially increasing the number of foes the party must overcome.

4   The adventurers encounter an ancient dragon which has been cursed by the Lord of Slime. The dragon no longer possesses its normal breath weapon, but instead vomits forth an array of various slimes and oozes in its place.

5   Intelligent monsters on one of the dungeon's levels harvest and contain a common form of ooze in pottery jars. They utilize these jars as missile weapons, hurling them at interlopers, or use the jars in traps which shatter the pottery and dump the ooze atop the unwary.

6   The party must traverse a section of damp dungeon corridors. Because of the wet walls, floors, and ceilings, it becomes difficult to spot the oozes and slimes that dwell within these hallways. Grey ooze is indistinguishable from mere wet stone and a patch of damp moss or lichen might actually be green slime.

7   A fountain of mysterious origin lies within the dungeon. At regular intervals, this fountain produces gouts of one or more types of oozes, jellies, or puddings that then creep off to seek sustenance in the dungeon. If the fountain can be destroyed or shut off, the party can restrict the number of these creatures encountered.

8   As part of an experiment's mishap or an arcane defensive measure, soap-like bubbles float through the dungeon hallways. Encapsulated within each bubble is a type of ooze, jelly or pudding in stasis. Should the bubble be punctured (a very easy task), the ooze is freed from containment and stasis, and is very, very hungry.

9   An ooze dwells inside a reservoir normally set aside for potable water (stone cistern, drinking fountain, or pump-activated well). When the adventurer attempts to draw water from the container, he finds himself in for a nasty surprise.

10   Little thought is given to the ooze after it is dispatched, but one mad genius has found a use for this nutrient-rich proto-matter. In vats and tanks located deep in the dungeon's depth, this insane biologist grows strange new life forms in an electrically charged primordial soup of dead oozes.

IS ALSO FOR OMEN

Omens, supernaturally-produced signs and portents indicating future events, are occasionally glimpsed by adventurers—far more so than those who pursue more mundane occupations. Due to their frequent delving into strange locales rife with mystical energies, adventurers regularly skirt the boundaries between the earthly and the spiritual. Adventurers who pursue aims of a higher nature—the service of a deity or the quest to right a horrible wrong—witness omens more frequently than those driven by simple avarice or bloodlust. The ineffable powers beyond the earthly veil step forth to provide guidance to these worthies, assisting them in their efforts.

Not all omens are the product of spirits or godly powers, however. Some mortal magics can conjure up glimpses into the future to provide guidance. The signs these magical incantations produce are cryptic and of limited knowledge, but can nevertheless provide insight when the proper (or less lethal) course of action needs to be determined. Omens invoked by mortal magic are less reliable than divinely-inspired ones, and wise conjurers know never to place their full trust in their own auguries. This allows the game master the opportunity to cloud the future and provides a convenient excuse when events don't necessarily unfold as anticipated.

A DOZEN ODD OMENS

D12   An Omen...

1   A portion of the caster's divination tools (runes, tarot cards, joss sticks, etc.) burst into uncanny flames, rot before his eyes, turn black and scorched, or are otherwise lost. The destroyed implements are those pointing towards a treacherous path, unwise course of action, or lethal decision. The tools linked to a less lethal choice remain unharmed.

2   The party discovers the dead bodies of another group of adventurers. The corpses are of equal number to the party and contain the exact same composition of the group's races and professions. Even their personal possessions closely resemble those of the party. The slain adventurers are discovered at an important juncture in the living party's quest, and are found closest to the most dangerous path.

3   A ghostly figure is seen by one or more of the party. The spirit bears horrific injuries (acid burns, rending claws marks, blood-drained pallor, etc.) inflicted by a formidable creature in the party's path. If the party takes heed of the figure, they can properly prepare for what lies in wait.

4   One member of the party sees phantasmal injuries or death signs on his compatriots. These injuries or death marks appear on his fellows most unprepared for what lies ahead (or most likely to perish in an encounter). Only the chosen PC witnesses the illusion, and it persists so long as the party maintains their current course of action. The vision fades if they turn aside from danger.

5   A single spell prepared by one of the party's casters reverberates or throbs in his mind as if demanding to be cast. The spell is one beneficial to the party in an event about to occur (a fire resistance spell as they approach a flame demon's lair, for example). If cast beforehand, the spell grants the party an increased chance of avoiding death or injury in the forthcoming encounter.

6   Naturally-occurring markings on the dungeon walls (niter deposits, mold, mineral striations, etc.) seem to depict symbols or images. These marks foreshadow a creature or trap situated ahead of the party and can be either clear depictions or cryptic hints. If the marks are defaced in any manner, the forthcoming encounter increases in difficulty.

7   The party's shadows, regardless of their light sources' positions, recoil from a specific direction. The shadows grow shorter or vanish entirely depending on the threat located in the indicated direction. Changing course away from the threat causes the shadows to return.

8   The caster's mouth fills with an abnormal taste upon casting his divination. Depending on the outcome of his prediction, the taste might be fair (the metallic taste of precious metals) or foul (ashes and blood). The taste lingers, intensifies, or vanishes depending on the future actions and directions of the party.

9   The party's torches behave strangely, throwing their flames in a direction against the draught or changing the strength of their brightness. The flames either guide the party towards beneficial discoveries or warn against danger. Through careful observation of the flames, the party can determine how close the encounter is and the size of its threat or windfall.

10   A recently slain opponent stirs briefly, raising its head up to speak cryptic prophecy to the party. The words may be a warning of what lies ahead, its body a temporary conduit of supernatural agents working in the group's favor, or the adversary's postmortem portent of the doom they are sure to suffer for their murderous crime.

11   The party's equipment manifests strange hints of events about to come. A pending encounter with a monster unharmed by ordinary weapons might result in traces of rust appearing on a warrior's sword, while a fiendish undead creature or evil object in the party's future causes the priest's holy water to glow with divine radiance.

12   A response to the caster's augury manifests in the innocuous statements of his confederates. The supernatural replies appear mixed into the ordinary speech of others, who are unaware of speaking them. A question as to which direction to venture may be heard by the caster as "Shall we go east *FOR SLITHERING DEATH LIES WAITING DOWN THE WESTERN STAIRS?*" In this example, the speaker has no memory of, nor himself hears, talk of the slithering menace. This omen requires collaboration between the game master and speaking player, but can be extremely effective and unsettling if done properly.

IS FOR POOLS

Deep under the earth, pools of liquids both unusual and mundane form in the darkness. Some are the result of intelligent hands, contained within low walls of worked brick and stone. Others form by natural circumstances, seeping out from the rocky walls and floors of **Caves**. Often strange of hue or form, these pools are natural watering holes for the denizens of the dungeon depths and serve as hunting grounds for predators or neutral ground for intelligent humanoid tribes. When filled with potable water, these pools are clear and clean; a welcomed sight for lost adventurers and a reminder of the sunlit lands above. Sometimes these waters are tainted by minerals, causing ordinary water to appear in a rainbow of hues and possess odd odors or tastes. Other times, the weird coloration indicates a poisonous brew. A party without a druid in their ranks may be forced to risk it all by just going ahead and sampling the pool's contents.

More often than not, however, these placid pools contain mysteries of a much deeper depth. Many possess strange powers, altering those who dare to taste of their waters. Some are benevolent, healing the wounds incurred during the adventure. Others are more sinister, causing ability scores to change radically, saving throws against poison to be made, or damage to be suffered. More than one unlucky adventurer has found that what appears to be a refreshing pool of water is in truth a caustic acid.

Even when the contents of these pools are harmless, the pools themselves may host threats to life and limb. Cavernous pools are where the giant crayfish live: albino, blind and hungry. The waters of a plain-looking well surge to life as a water weird rises from its depths. The rotting vegetable matter in a natural spring is actually a colony of throat leeches. The party must judge on its own whether the possible boons of these pools outweigh their threats.

D10 Roll	TEN RANDOM POOL PROPERTIES (5% Chance Per Dungeon Level)
1	Pool is of unusual content: 1 – Salt water 2 – Wine 3 – Vinegar 4 – Acid 5 – Green slime 6 – Pitch/oil 7 – Blood 8 – Treasure (real or illusionary) 9 – Unidentified viscous liquid 10 – Gaseous vapor
2	Pool is of unusual form: 1 – Fountain 2 – Cistern 3 – Well 4 – Reflecting pool 5 – Bathing pool 6 – Aquatic animal tank
3	Pool teleports anyone entering it to another location.
4	Pool contains life: 1 – Ordinary fish 2 – Giant crayfish or 3 – catfish 4 – Throat leeches 5 – Water weird 6 – Giant crab 7 – Nixies/Selkies/Kelpies 8 – Cave piranha
5	Pool is of an odd color: 1 – Green 2 – Purple 3 – Yellow 4 – Aquamarine 5 – Red 6 – Orange
6	Pool is poisonous. Death to all who drink from it.
7	Pool is sentient. May speak to the party, answer questions, beg favors, grant spells, etc.
8	Water in the pool is magically "sharp." Stepping into it or pouring it on the skin cuts like razors (1d6 points of damage).
9	Pool recharges any magic item that relies on charges/uses which is placed into it. One-time only effect.
10	Pool heals those who enter or drink from it. This magical healing may heal damage, cure poisons or diseases, remove curses, cure insanity, regenerate lost limbs, etc. as determined by the referee.

IS ALSO FOR POTIONS

Potions—those enchanted elixirs of concentrated power—are often a novice adventurer's first taste of magic in the early days of his adventuring career. In some places, potions are a common type of magic item, available for sale in dusty alchemist shops and evil-smelling witches' tents. On other worlds where magic is rarer, potions are first encountered on the shelves in wizard's lairs or stashed at the bottom of a rotting backpack still attached to the skeletal remains of its previous owner. Wherever they are found, potions are greatly prized by adventurers for both their portability and potability.

These mystical drinks are more than just liquid magic; they are also a test of nerve. Most potions are found lacking clear labels, requiring their acquirers to sample them directly to determine their powers. Alas, not all potions are beneficial. Some are lethal poisons that kill with the slightest taste. More than one veteran adventurer has died when that serene blue elixir he believed to be a curative draught turned out to be highly toxic. Wise adventuring bands are known to test a suspect potion on livestock acquired for that sole purpose when unmarked elixirs are discovered.

Potions come in an endless variety of colors, effervescence, taste, smell, and consistency—no two are alike, which adds to the difficulty of identifying them. Potions are also not always consumable and various oils, unguents, powders, and salves regularly share the powers of elixirs. The containers they are found in are as varied as their contents and one can tell an experienced adventurer by the assortment of vials, philters, jars, bottles, flasks, and beakers he accumulates throughout his career. Some are kept as curios; other retained for the purpose of refilling them the next time an alchemist's den is discovered in the dungeon's depths.

A SCORE OF PUZZLING POTIONS

D20	The potion is...
1	In dried form. Seemingly colorful dust, if the powder is mixed with a liquid it becomes a typical magical potion. Some dried potions require liquids other than water to mix properly, including wine, holy water, urine, or freshly spilled blood.
2	Horrible tasting. The drinker must make a resistance roll to keep the potion down after drinking it. On a failed roll, the drinker vomits up the elixir, losing its benefits.
3	Sentient. As an odd side-effect of its brewing, the potion is semi-intelligent and has no desire to be consumed. Those attempting to drink the potion must make an agility roll to swallow it before it leaps from the bottle and flows away as fast as it can. It screams as it is drunk.
4	Full of glittering fragments. Like a popular liqueur, flecks of gold or other precious metal are suspended in the potion. These particles are solely for decoration or taste and can be filtered out of the elixir without affecting its potency. The precious flakes are worth 50 gold pieces.
5	The product of its container. While the potion itself is magical, the bottle, flask, or other container it comes in is even more so. Anytime pure water or another liquid of the referee's choosing is poured into the bottle, it transforms into a random magical potion. The container may have a limit on the amount of transformations it can produce before losing its magic.
6	Addictive. Anyone consuming the potion must make a resistance check or become addicted to that type of potion. They will expend a fortune acquiring more of that potion variety and drink them even when there is no need for their magical benefits. An addict who fails to drink his potion of choice at least once each week suffers penalties to attack, skill, and resistance rolls until he consumes another draught of the elixir.
7	Gelatinous. The potion has turned semi-solid and can no longer be drunk normally. It must be eaten with a spoon or, in dire cases, snorted up the nose. It is otherwise unchanged. Some fiendish dungeon lords acquire gelatinous potions to seed their delves, allowing intruders to become accustomed to this strange variety of elixir. Then, went least expected, a lethal jelly or gelatinous beast is bottled and left for invaders to discover.
8	Unusually administered. Rather than a bottled liquid, the potion is found in a hypodermic syringe, pill form, or as a dermal patch. The drink functions normally and only its manner of consumption is changed. Depending on the base level of technological development in the campaign, the PCs might need to make skill or intelligence checks to figure out how to use the potion.
9	Produces strange side-effects. Consuming the elixir invokes its power as normal but also causes weird reactions in the drinker's body. A potion that protects against fire turns the drinker's skin bright red; a curative concoction causes his body to glow blue for a short duration; or a potion of invisibility makes his spoken words visible in the air around him.
10	Of varied potency. Due to either age or the brewer's skill, the potion might be more or less powerful than is typical. An older potion might last half the normal duration, while a stronger elixir lasts twice as long.
11	A bizarre concoction. Perhaps the result of an apprentice's mistake or the last-ditch effort by an adventurer in dire straits, the potion combines two effects in a single draught. A potion of great potency might also heal its drinker, or a potion of flight could turn the PC invisible as well. The two mixed potions should be determined randomly. Potions that cancel one another out still radiate a magical dweomer but produce no discernable effect when consumed. Alchemists and wizards would pay handsomely to possess such a drink so they might analyze it and duplicate the recipe.
12	Affects multiple creatures. When consumed, the potion's magic takes effect in a 10-foot radius around the drinker, granting its benefits (or hazards) to any creature within that area. The potion's effects, if of random strength or duration, are rolled for each affected target.
13	Mildly poisonous. Consuming the potion requires the drinker to make a resistance check against toxins. If this roll is failed, the drinker experiences discomfort and nausea as the liquid works its way through his system. This mild poisoning manifests as penalties to attack rolls, skill checks, and resistance rolls, and may even affect spell casting at the referee's discretion. The potion otherwise works as intended, and the nausea can be relieved with the appropriate curative magics, substances, or skills.
14	Can reproduce itself. So long as the entire potion is not consumed when used, whatever small amount remains reproduces itself in 1d6 days if placed within a suitable container. The drinker must state at the time of consumption that he is not drinking the entire elixir and likely suffers a reduction to the potion's duration or effect in return. This reproductive property may be limited, or recreated potions might have their potency reduced exponentially.
15	Mislabeled. Although most potions are found without any form of visible identification, some still bear yellowed labels identifying their contents. This potion has such markings, but due to honest error or sheer maliciousness, the label is incorrect. A party naïve enough to take such markings at face value are in for a shock when the liquid is consumed.
16	Contains magic-eating parasites. The potion is infested with microscopic organisms that feed on magical energy. These parasites are harmless to non-spell casting creatures but thrive inside magic-wielding ones. A spell caster who drinks the potion becomes infected with the organisms. Until cured, all spells cast suffer a minor reduction in power (-1 to damage, last 1 time unit less than normal, etc.). Curative or dispelling magics will rid the caster of his undesired guests.
17	In another state. The potion might be gaseous or solid, constrained within the confines of its bottle. In order to be consumed safely, the party must find a way to alter its physical state. This could be as simple as heating or cooling the potion, or it might require dramatic steps to bring about the change.
18	Affects only certain races. The potion was especially brewed to respond to the particular metabolism of a specific race or species. All other races drinking the draught are unaffected by the potion or might suffer wildly unpredictable results. Some clue can be found on the potion bottle identifying the race for which it is meant, but these markings are likely to be cryptic and require special knowledge or spells to decipher.
19	In component parts. The potion is discovered in three separate containers, each holding a special reagent that reacts with the others to form a conglomerate elixir. The order in which they are mixed may or may not matter, but if it does, mixing the reagents in the wrong order is likely to cause explosive results.
20	Locked. The potion's stopper is sealed in some manner, usually by a key- or combination-lock. The container itself is magically treated and is stronger than steel, making it near impossible to break open. In order to access the draught, the appropriate key or combination must be found or special magics or larcenous skills employed.

IS FOR QUESTIONS

The dungeon is the home of mysteries. Despite whatever rumors and legends that may have been acquired in the safety of inns, taverns, and the marketplace, once the doors of the dungeon have been breached, the party has entered the undiscovered country. The questions they discover once within the dank confines of the dungeon may run the gamut from the simple to the unknowable, but each begs an answer.

At the very least, questions such as "what's behind those doors?" or "what may we find down those stairs?" play through the minds of the adventurers. However, as they probe the depths, more complex queries begin to arise. "Who built this place and is he/she/it still lurking in its depths?" "What happens if we place this rod into that slot we discovered?" "What is making that horrible scream?" "Are you really who you say you are?" A good dungeon should always pose more questions than it answers. The attempts to unlock all a dungeon's secrets will ensure that the adventurers continue to risk their lives in search of answers.

EIGHT QUESTIONS TO KEEP THE ADVENTURERS GUESSING

D8 Roll	
1	One of the party's henchmen goes missing. After a short time, he is either found or returns. When questioned, he has no memory of the events of the past hour. Spells and similar methods of inquiry reveal nothing untoward. What happened to him and is he still who he seems to be?
2	The party chances upon an oversized stone disk, marked with increments, and slowly turning. After thorough examination, it becomes clear that this is a timer, counting down to some event. What happens when time runs out?
3	The adventurers find the personal belongings and equipment of another adventuring party. This gear shows no signs of damage or wear. The clothing and armor is fastened tight, as if the wearers were somehow removed from their apparel without disturbing its buttons, straps, or lashings. It's as if they just vanished from their clothing and belongings. What could do this?
4	Several times during their foray, the party spies a small glowing eye hovering in the air nearby. The eye simply observes their explorations, battles, and activities, never coming too close to their position. It disappears if the party approaches it, only to reappear later on. Who or what is keeping tabs on the adventurers?
5	A hallway or room abruptly ends in unworked stone, as if construction was suddenly abandoned. Was it caused by the death of the dungeon's builder, a dangerous discovery by his workers, or some other unknown reason? Perhaps the room or hall only appears to end, but secretly continues concealed by magic, hidden panels, or even into another plane of existence.
6	As the party explores the dungeon, they continually find clues and warnings left specifically for them. These clues include messages written on walls, notes stuck in between loose stones and marked intersections of hallways. Someone appears to be looking out for them, but who and why?
7	The party notes a sudden change in the appearance of the dungeon. The stonework and architecture is much older here, indicating that this section predated the rest of the complex. What purpose did this ancient underground area serve? Did the builder(s) of the newer section know of its existence… and is this older complex still home to whatever originally dwelled within?
8	Throughout the dungeon stand several doors that have been sealed and locked by obviously magical means. Each bears old symbols that allude to great dangers contained within each. These doors resist all efforts to open them or detect what lies beyond. In time the party discovers an ornate key that seems to fit the locks on each door. Do they dare to use it?

IS ALSO FOR QUESTS

Many an adventurer enters the dungeon with no higher goal than to fill his or her pouches with plunder or to liberate ancient magical objects from the skeletal grasp of their previous owners. Some, however, have nobler purposes in mind—a solemn vow to uphold, a religious pilgrimage to fulfill, or a catastrophe to avert or end.

Still other adventurers have quests forced upon them, finding themselves bound to pursue a goal by magical compulsion. Spells such as *geas* or *quest* override the free will of afflicted adventurers, demanding they dedicate themselves to fulfilling their enforced compulsion if they ever want to escape magical control.

Fourteen Random Dungeon Quest Givers

D14   The party recieves a quest from...

1   A talking animal. The beast may be inherently magical or a creature transformed into another form.

2   A restless un-dead being whose tomb the party has defiled.

3   A cursed tome documenting the author's attempts to fulfill some important task. The writer perished before completing the quest and now anyone reading the text must take up his duty.

4   A fallen angel seeking atonement.

5   An enchanted weapon that delivers an ultimately fatal wound upon the quest recipient. The wound does not heal unless the quest is fulfilled and time is running out for the injured character.

6   The still-beating heart of a dead god or other powerful entity.

7   A desperate group of refugees dwelling at the end of the time stream who seek to reverse some terrible catastrophe in the PC's era.

8   An insane alchemist who can inject magical compulsions in others via his weird techno-magical contraptions.

9   An utterly nondescript rock.

10   A bejeweled reliquary containing the bones of a holy saint or an unholy apostate.

11   The lingering, physically manifested dreams of a deceased paladin who perished in pursuit of their holy vow.

12   A lowly goblin witch doctor armed with powerful, charming juju dust.

13   The dungeon itself places a compulsion on all who reach its heart.

Fourteen Random Quests to Fulfill

D14 **The character/party must...**

1   Locate a long-lost magical or religious artifact.

2   Bury the mortal remains of a hero at some distant or nearly inaccessible location (another plane, the lair of a powerful monster, on a permanently storm-swept mountain top, etc.)

3   Procure seven sacred hairs from the head of an angel or nine blasphemous fingernails from the hands of a devil.

4   Insult a mighty warrior, powerful potentate, or demigod to their face.

5   Close a portal leading to another world or dimension before a terrible menace can emerge.

6   Slay every firstborn child in a village to appease a Chaos Lord.

7   Save an entire village from a horrible agent of evil determined to decimate the town.

8   Collect a drop of liquid from each of the world's seas and purify a sacred object with their mingled waters.

9   Assassinate a well-respected noble to start a war

10   Defeat a champion of Law, Chaos, or Neutrality to adjust the Cosmic Balance.

11   Gift all one's worldly possessions to a specific group in need.

12   Resurrect a long-dead hero or villain in the name of justice long-deferred.

13   Erect a temple or fortress in the name of a religious figure or military leader.

14   Serve as a guardian to the quest giver until a specific obligation is fulfilled (the character saves the quest-giver's life three times, for a period of a year and a day, until the character finds another who agrees to take on the burden, etc.)

IS FOR ROOMS

Without rooms, there are only **Hallways** — and those do not a dungeon make. From bare chambers to cluttered libraries, rooms come in all shapes and sizes. Some sport high, vaulted ceilings, their tops lost in the gloom beyond the torch light. Others are tiny spaces, restricting movement and lines of retreat. Many still bear clues as to what their original purpose may have been, holding rotted furniture and decayed *objects d'art*. But in some, time and the actions of the dungeon's inhabitants have erased all traces of the room's original intent, leaving only plain stone and the traces of the creatures' presence. Either purposely placed or randomly created, the room is where the dungeon truly comes to life, often to the chagrin of the explorers.

As with most other features of the dungeon, rooms often contain mysteries or unseen dangers. Some rise or fall, depositing the party on a level they wished not to explore. Some are the homes of creatures that blend into the stones of the room, seeming to be a harmless part of the construction. The widow of the adventurer lost to a trapper or the orphan of one brought low by a lurker above will tell you to fear those harmless looking floors and ceilings. Even the walls have been known to spring into action, grinding closer and closer together as the party struggles to halt their advance. On rare occasions, some rooms serve as impenetrable redoubts of safety and respite for the weary party. Strange magics secure the doors from outside interruption or even accelerate the cycle of time within its walls, allowing for rest and re-memorization of spells at a fraction of the normal required time. These rooms are the exception rather than the rule, however, and should be coveted whenever found.

2d10 Roll	RANDOM ROOMS AND CHANCY CHAMBERS
2	Extra dimensional room — Room's interior is of much greater size than the surrounding area would seem to allow.
3	Redoubt — Room can be sealed to provide an area of safe rest for the party. No wandering monsters are encountered.
4	Carnivorous room — Hidden danger lurks in the room disguised as normal furnishings, walls, floor, or ceiling.
5	Elevator room — Room ascends/descends between two or more levels.
6	Tesseract — Room is a four-dimensional hypercube.
7	Environment room — Room is designed to be habitable by a creature accustomed to an uncommon environment. Examples are fire room, ice room, water room, vacuum chamber, etc.
8	Siphon room — Room drains health, memorized spells, magical charges, life levels, etc. for every ten minutes spent within it. Energy might power nefarious devices or be stored for later use.
9	Silent room — Room silences any sound made or produced within its walls.
10	Miniature room — Room has been built to accommodate creatures of a much smaller size. Ceiling is low, doors are small, and all furnishings are built on a small scale.
11	Strange gravity — Room is filled with a zero-gravity or reverse-gravity field.
12	Puzzle room — Walls, doors, and other features of the room shift and slide, blocking the entrance, creating new exits, or uncovering hidden secrets.
13	Spell amplifier — Spells cast while in this room produce the maximum effects possible.
14	Rotating room — Room spins unnoticed when door closes, allowing access to another dungeon area and possibly confusing mapping attempts.
15	Accelerated time room — When the door to this room is closed, time inside passes at a rate of 24 hours for each hour that passes outside.
16	Stasis room — Any living creature in this room enters a state of stasis when the door is sealed. The creature no longer requires food or drink or ages. Stasis can only be ended by opening the door from the outside.
17	Peace room — Room's enchantment prevents any acts of violence from occurring within it. Creatures encountered in this room are more likely to be friendly and helpful to the party.
18	One-way room — Room possesses two doors, one at each end. Room may only be entered from one and only exited from the other.
19	Static electricity room — The atmosphere of this chamber is heavily charged with static electricity, which discharges when living creatures touch metal or one another, causing a small amount of damage.
20	Compacting room — walls or ceiling slowly grind close to crush anyone inside.

RANDOM ORIGINAL PURPOSE OF ROOMS & CHAMBERS

These tables are composed of diverse types of rooms likely to be found within a dungeon setting, divided into categories based on the functions of said rooms. All that is required to use the table is a percentile roll on a single master chart, followed by subsequent roll of a variable dice type on an associated sub-table. These tables may be used to determine what function a dungeon room originally or currently serves, giving the referee a better idea as to what might be found in that room when fleshing it out in his or her notes.

Table 1 - Room Category

D%	Table Result
01-03	Audience - *Sub-Table A*
04-08	Captivity - *Sub-Table B*
09-15	Entertainment - *Sub-Table C*
16-25	Functional - *Sub-Table D*
26-60	General - *Sub-Table E*
61-65	Military - *Sub-Table F*
66-70	Religious - *Sub-Table G*
71-75	Scholarly - *Sub-Table H*
76-00	Utility - *Sub-Table I*

Sub-Table A — Audience Rooms

D8	Room
1-3	Amphitheater
4-5	Audience Chamber
6	Court Room
7	Hall, Great
8	Throne Room

Sub-Table B — Captivity Rooms

D6	Room
1	Bestiary/Zoo
2-3	Cell, Prison
4	Kennel
5-6	Pen/Prison

Sub-Table C — Entertainment Rooms

D10	Room
1-2	Banquet Chamber
3-4	Game Room
5	Harem/Seraglio
6-7	Music Room
8	Torture Chamber
9-10	Trophy Room

Sub-Table D — Functional Rooms

D10	Room
1	Gallery
2	Hall
3-4	Lounge
5-6	Reception Chamber
7-8	Salon
9-10	Sitting Room

Sub-Table E — General Purpose Rooms

D20	Room
1-2	Antechamber
3-6	Bedroom, Average
7-8	Bedroom, Elite
9	Cistern
10	Dressing Room
11	Privy
12-13	Servant's Dormitory
14-17	Storage
18-20	Waiting Room

Sub-Table F — Military Rooms

D6	Room
1	Armory
2-3	Barracks
4-5	Guard Room
6	Training/Exercise Room

Sub-Table G — Religious Rooms

D12	Room
1-2	Cell, Monk
3	Chantry
4	Chapel
5-6	Crypt
7-8	Meditation Chamber
9	Robing Room/Vestry
10	Confessional
11	Scriptorium
12	Shrine

Sub-Table H — Scholarly Rooms

D20	Room
1-2	Classroom
3	Conjuring Room
4	Divination Chamber
5-6	Laboratory
7-9	Library
10	Observatory
11-12	Office
13-16	Study
17-20	Workshop

Sub-Table I — Utility Rooms

D12	Room
1	Bath
2	Closet
3-4	Dining Room
5-6	Kitchen
7-8	Meeting Chamber
9-10	Office
11-12	Pantry

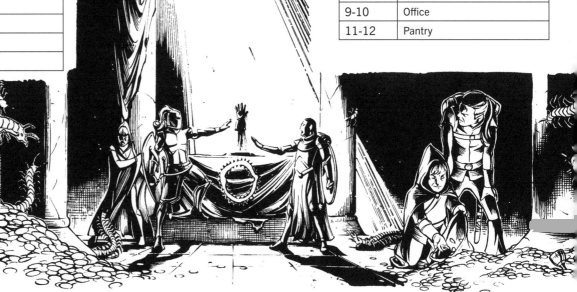

IS ALSO FOR RELICS

As self-centered as many professional adventurers can be, some grudgingly admit that history does not begin with their own exploits and that they are merely the latest link in a chain that extends far back into the mists of time. And like many other human endeavors, the history of dungeon exploration (or as less kind souls call it, "tomb robbery") has left its mark upon the physical world. These marks take the form of relics: material evidence of those who have come previously.

Relics can take many forms. In some cases, relics are simply an object or proof of presence left behind by past adventurers. At other times, relics are actual body parts of living creatures preserved for posterity. It is rare for an adventuring community to lack a "patron saint of adventurers," usually either a minor demi-god or a legendary explorer whose exploits are still told around the taproom. Either of these types of relics can possess special powers. Sometimes these weird properties are divine in nature. Other times it is the bad luck that plagued the relic's previous owner lingering around the item.

Experienced adventurers take careful note of any relics discovered during their delvings. An abundance of burnt-out torch stubs indicate the current section of the dungeon is thoroughly explored and unlikely to contain riches or magic. A large bloodstain and crushed bones is a sure sign that a collapsing ceiling trap stands in the party's path. A carefully preserved hand wrapped in expensive cloth and ensconced in a decorated coffer must certainly possess unique properties or value to the right people. The discovery and recovery of relics can even be the goal of a dungeon expedition. Religious zealots will pay handsomely to obtain a physical part of their revered leader, and a wealthy family would reward those who returned to them the body (or portion thereof) of their beloved, but ne'er do-well son who perished in a dungeon.

TEN RANDOM PATRON SAINTS OF ADVENTURE AND THE POWER OF THEIR RELICS

D10	The adventuring saint is...
1	St. Ardmis the Cunning. In life this rogue performed the Nine Mysterious Robberies still spoken of in thieves' guilds across the realm. His mummified hand puts anyone within a single structure into a magical sleep lasting twelve hours.
2	St. Obliantuk the Bold. This fighter held the Bridge of Frozen Tears against the demon army of Frikk. When he died at the age of 106, his ten loyal bodyguards each took one of Obliantuk's toes as instructed. Anyone bearing one of these digits cannot be forced to flee from battle and is nearly impossible to overbear or knockdown.
3	St. Nicodemus the Loyal. An unconventional saint, Nicodemus was the mule companion of the Society of Foolish Fops who rescued them by dragging the band to the surface after being overcome by the Pustule Fumes of Drantil. One of Nicodemus' vertebra grants its owner the ability to carry superhuman loads without slowing down.
4	St. Kullcos the Always Ready. Renowned for his magical bags that contained anything an adventuring band could ever need, it's said he who carries a lock of Kullcos' hair always finds the right tool for the job lying around at the moment he requires it.
5	St. Ellenimee the Swift. Ellenimee survived the Gauntlet of Blades in the Tomb of Grongar, a task no mortal has ever repeated. Her fingernails are said to grant boosts of speed to their bearers when unexpected danger threatens.
6	St. Wrengen the Stained. Wrengen was famous in life for his precise maps and ink-stained hands. Those who obtain one of his shriveled, ink-splattered fingers know a room's dimensions with complete accuracy at a glance and are always aware of the direction they travel.
7	St. Orumocculus the All-Seeing. Orumocculus was blind in life, but nevertheless had a supernatural knack for discerning secret doors and hidden traps. He who owns one of the saint's petrified eyeballs gains the ability to see these same secret constructions.
8	St. Illyrissa the Glib. Said to be able to charm the scales off a dragon, Illyrissa possessed a melodious voice and uncanny knowledge of etiquette and debate. The owner of her incorrupt tongue shares these same gifts.
9	St. Ruul the Greater. Famed for building the Adamantine Golem of Hrusk and its subsequent victory over the armies of the Nefarious Potentates, Ruul had a gift for locating and deciphering rare magics thought lost forever. Tufts of his black beard are said to bolster any magical endeavor brushed with their ebony bristles.
10	St. Kerennimeth the Resolved. Kerennimeth walked into the Necropolis of Hate and smote the undead legions that garrisoned it. The ribs which sheltered her stout heart in life now grant their owners an aegis against the chilling touch of the dead and gift them with increased power to turn away or destroy the restless dead with divine energy.

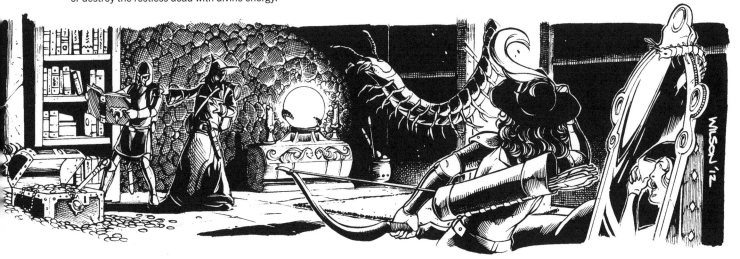

THIRTY RANDOM RELICS FROM PREVIOUS ADVENTURERS

D30	The relic is...
1	The skeletal remains of a humanoid creature. A rotting wooden stake has been driven through its ribcage. Do the PCs dare remove it?
2	A battered lantern enchanted with a permanent illumination spell. The lantern hangs suspended in the air with no means of support.
3	A pitted short sword with a gauntlet wrapped around its hilt. The gauntlet contains a severed human hand. If the sword is grasped, visions of painful death assail the PC who holds it.
4	An iron spike driven into the floor. A hemp rope is tied to the spike and leads around a corner. At the opposite end the rope is twisted into a noose, slick with blood.
5	A game piece from a popular gambling house or other such venue. A personalized inscription is carved upon it. Carrying the item brings its owner a streak of misfortune.
6	A pair of worn but serviceable high, hard boots. The boots squeak when worn and attract wandering monsters.
7	A burned and water-stained spellbook containing 1d4 random spells. The final page contains a suicide note.
8	A crude cairn of stone with a steel breastplate acting as a grave marker. A name, date, and brief obituary are scratched into the breastplate. The cairn has been disturbed and is empty.
9	A scratched and chipped glass eye. It has no magical properties but always appears to be staring at whoever first discovered it.
10	A pile of discarded ration wrappings and empty waterskins. Mixed amongst the heap are refilled containers and wrappings holding human blood and dwarf meat.
11	A pair of dead and maggot-ridden guard dogs. Their leather barding remains intact and is curiously free of weapon-damage.
12	A simple sketch map of the immediate dungeon drawn on a wall in chalk. Unbeknownst to the PCs, the map is incorrect and leads those following it into hidden dangers.
13	Several smashed holy water vials and a gnawed-off human finger in a pool of blood. The blood refuses to coagulate and dry.
14	A warning written in blood and bearing an odd, possibly occult symbol. The symbol is the sign of a secret brotherhood of dungeon explorers and the warning a passphrase known only by its members.
15	An expensive spell component seemingly dropped accidentally from a passing wizard's pouch. The component is slightly defective and was purposely thrown away.
16	A necklace made from "trophies" (ears, teeth, or other bodily parts) collected from slain humanoid creatures. If worn, encounters with those same creatures always turn violent once they glimpse the grim necklace.
17	A worn-down whetstone on a rawhide thong. Edged weapons sharpened with the stone gain a bonus to attack rolls and damage, but fumbled attacks always inflict damage on the weapon's wielder.
18	A cheap locket containing the portrait of a man or woman. Whoever claims the locket is haunted by the ghost of the necklace's previous owner who badgers the PC to find the person depicted in the portrait and give the locket to him/her.
19	A bent iron holy symbol dedicated to the god of luck. Clerics using this item invoke the whim of that capricious deity when attempting to affect the undead. Roll 1d6 to determine its effect each time it is used: (1) suffer a -2/-10% penalty; (2) suffer a -1/-5% penalty; (3-4) no effect; (5) add a +1/+5% bonus; (6) add a +2/+10% bonus.
20	A cracked bone whistle tied to a piece of string. Blowing the whistle produces no audible result to human and demi-human ears but attracts vermin and certain humanoid creatures of the referee's choice.
21	A "scarecrow" crafted from the bones and belongings of a slain adventurer. It turns to watch the party as they pass, chuckling eerily all the while.
22	A rusty set of thieves' tools fused together by intense heat. One of the picks in the mass is of exceptional quality, granting a +2/+10% bonus when used in conjunction with larcenous skills. Unless extracted carefully, however, it becomes damaged and reverts to a normal implement.
23	A grapnel hanging from a ring in the ceiling. Rotting meat is attached to one of its tines. A black-painted cord, difficult to see in the dungeon gloom, stretches off into the hands of a lurking monster using the hook as a subterranean fishing lure.
24	A sealed, scuffed leather scroll case. If opened, gray ash is found inside. The ashes are the burned remains of a slain adventurer collected in the hopes of raising him from the dead.
25	A battered steel helmet, inverted and affixed to a stem of bone. Encrusted with blood, the helmet was fashioned into a ceremonial goblet used by a dark cult and then lost.
26	A steaming mound of monster waste. Those giving it more than a passing glance notice the skull, partially digested equipment, and other remaining parts of an adventurer who met his end as the monster's most recent meal.
27	A battle-axe lodged in the skull of a gigantic beast. The axe's shaft is broken, but the head is salvageable if it can be pried from the skull's bony hold. If repaired, the axe is of the slaying variety against the creature in whose corpse it was discovered but always misses foes of any other type.
28	A pried-up flagstone, chipped by tools and set aside. Beneath it is a hollow showing signs of once containing a large chest. A dead hireling with a dagger in his back now fills the hole. If taken, the dagger always turns on its owner until buried in the back of a trusted ally.
29	A half-empty bottle filled with a fine and rare spirit. Anyone sampling this liquid runs the risk of attracting its former (and now-deceased) owner's attention, granting the imbiber either a small boon of luck or a curse for drinking the liquor when its original owner can no longer enjoy it.
30	A damaged lute lacking strings. It is of quality construction and can be repaired. If restored, the first person playing it sings a tune of lost treasure and secret magic hidden far away. They've never heard this song before and have no inkling why they sang it.

IS FOR STATUES

In the shadowy chambers and corridors of the dungeon, odd constructions stand as mute witnesses to the events that unfold before their lifeless eyes. Some have been erected to honor or pacify strange gods, while others are tributes to the vanity of Men. Whatever the case, these silent statues can be found throughout the dungeon depths. Most are carved from common forms of stone, their value lying only in the skill of their makers. Rarer statues are carved or cast from more valuable materials: gold, silver, platinum, onyx, obscure forms of marble, even mithral. Legends speak of one statue depicting the Scarlet King, crafted from a single ruby, yet standing the height of a man. Even those of common construction are sometimes adorned with giant **Jewels** to add to their luster and beauty. More than one party has come across a statue of tremendous value, only to find that they lack the tools, skills, or manpower to rescue it from the dungeon deep.

Some statues possess valuable traits that far outstrip the mere worth of their construction. These have been known to grant boons of fortune upon those who place offerings at their feet. Others turn dross metals into more valuable forms. Some grant wishes to those who touch them with bare hands when the stars are in the proper alignment.

Unfortunately, these beneficial statues have their diametrically opposed twins. Such harmful statues strip ability scores or even experience levels from those who touch them. Others lay potent curses upon would-be defilers of the sacred tombs the statues hold watch over. Another type springs to unholy life, spouting gouts of magma from their stony mouths or rays of intense heat from their sightless eyes.

Despite these horrors, not all statues that move are things to be feared. Some have been placed to allow entrance through gigantic doors. When the password is spoken aloud, these stone juggernauts grind slowly into action, opening the Cyclopean portals to grant access to the **Rooms** beyond. Other statues sit quietly with palms outstretched on the floor of a high vaulted chamber. When commanded, they stand erect, lifting the waiting party aloft in the palms of their hands and depositing them safely on a ledge high above.

HOW TO USE THIS TABLE

To randomly determine what type of statue is found in the dungeon roll a d20 twice. The first die result indicates what the statue depicts, while the second reveals what material it is constructed from. For example, the referee rolls a 5 and a 13, indicating the character discovers a glass or crystal statue of a young child. After determining what the statue is, the referee should check to see if it bears any special properties. If so, the referee rolls a third d20 and consults the table to determine what that property is. To continue our example, the referee rolls percentile dice to see if the statue has additional properties. Since the glass statue of the child is located on the third dungeon level, it has a 30% chance of such properties being present. A roll of 05 indicates that it has special properties. A third roll of the d20 comes up 4, showing that the statue recharges a magical item placed in its hands. The referee makes a note of this and describes the statue, when encountered, as having an outstretched arm with an upturned palm. What the players decide to do determines if they discover this additional feature.

D20 Roll	FIGURE DEPICTED	MADE FROM	SPECIAL PROPERTIES (10% CHANCE PER DUNGEON LEVEL)
1	Abstract form	Stone	Changes any who touch it into small, harmless animal.
2	Armored warrior	Stone	Will answer 1-3 questions about the dungeon.
3	Athlete	Stone	Imbues random party member with good fortune lasting 24 hours.
4	Bipedal monster	Stone	Recharges magical item placed in its hands.
5	Child	Stone	Animates and attacks interlopers.
6	Common animal	Bronze	Statue spews green slime or other ooze.
7	Couple – lovers, enemies engaged in a duel, etc.	Bronze	Points towards a trap, treasure, hidden clue, etc.
8	Demon or Devil	Bronze	Portion of statue missing – replacing missing component will result in a helpful/harmful effect (50/50 chance).
9	Dragon	Iron	Provides access to another section of the dungeon.
10	Famous entertainer	Iron	Ranged attack (throws lightning, heat rays, spits acid, shoots arrows, etc.).
11	Geometric shape or shapes	Wood	Contains hidden compartment filled with treasure.
12	Hooded, featureless figure	Wood	With proper command, animates and serves the party.
13	Inanimate object	Crystal/Glass	Statue is actually a living creature transformed by magic (cursed, enchanted, turned to stone, etc.).
14	Magic-user	Crystal/Glass	Acts as magical timepiece (casts shadows like a sundial, position of limbs indicate time, chimes each appointed hour, etc.).
15	Mounted figure	Brass	Dispenses magical potion, oil, or elixir.
16	Multiple figures – last stand of hero, surrounded by fallen foes; coronation of a king; druid and her animal companions, etc.	Silver	Statue is decorated with gems and/or jewels. Removing these may have dire consequences as determined by the referee.
17	Quadrupedal (or more) monster	Gold	Acts as recording device. If activated, replays images, speaks journal entries aloud, recites spell or prayers, etc.
18	Religious figure – deity, saint, angel, pious priest, etc.	Light – illusion or hologram	Causes magic cast in its presence to fizzle, rebound on caster, or produce random effect.
19	Ruler	Platinum	Statue's head/eyes follow the party's movements. Someone or something may be observing them…
20	Worker or tradesman	Mithral	Statue sings, speaks, roars, or otherwise makes sounds.

Few things evoke a mixture of excitement and trepidation in dungeon explorers more than a newly discovered flight of stairs leading further into the dungeon's depths. On one hand, veteran adventurers know that a hitherto-unexplored dungeon level is likely to contain new treasures to enrich their coffers. Yet these same explorers are aware that deeper dungeon levels contain threats of greater lethality. Seldom does one descend a dungeon stairwell without thinking he might never be heard from again.

Most dungeon stairs are simple affairs hewn from the surrounding stone or crafted from hastily formed slabs of rock. Bare of decoration, they are created for the sole purpose of allowing dungeon residents access to other levels. But even these plain staircases are not without hazards. Stairs form natural chokepoints in the dungeon, slowing flight from danger and granting higher ground for enemies to fight from. Other staircases become the hunting grounds of lurking monsters, attracted by the steady flow of traffic between levels. A dusty and seemingly unused stairwell might be a forgotten and unguarded entrance to a new section of the dungeon or a trapped passage avoided by those creatures aware of its hazards.

Rare dungeon stairs are not formed from stone at all but stranger materials. A staircase crafted of solid ice leads to a dungeon level permanently frozen by powerful magics. Metal stairs might be affixed to hidden gears that make them rise or fall or be trapped by invisible but deadly electrical currents. Some stairs are organic, formed by the weird excretions of insectile races or built from the bones and rotting flesh of a necromancer's victims. Such odd staircases inevitably lead into danger, but the rewards awaiting the brave dungeon adventurers who descend them are often worth the risk.

UNUSUAL DUNGEON STAIRS

D20	The stairs...
1	Are "nightingale steps" specifically designed to emit groans or chirps when stepped on. These noises alert the monstrous guardians below that a meal in on its way.
2	Are alive. They might be crafted from flesh and bone and inhabited by the spirits of slain beings or possessed by creatures from the Elemental Plane of Earth. Depending on the stairs' attitude, these disembodied spirits can assist the party with information about what awaits below or be a potent threat to overcome, leaving the party to wonder how one does battle with a flight of stairs?
3	Are semi-solid. Each step is actually a trough filled with a viscous material such as mud, wet clay, or stranger substances. These clinging materials require the travelers to tread carefully along the edges of the steps to avoid the goop or to step boldly into it and risk caltrops, spikes, or hidden vermin. Travel up and down the stairs is slowed, making flight from dangerous foes a dicey proposition.
4	Have direction-muddling enchantments cast upon them. Anyone encountering the stairs sees them as leading in the direction opposite where they truly lead. This effect results in mapping errors or funnels the party into a place they really don't wish to visit.
5	Decrease in size as they descend. This might be a purely mundane effect designed to force explorers into single-file and to make combat difficult. It could also have a magical effect such as causing the party to shrink in size the further they go, resulting in 1-foot-tall adventurers by the time they reach the bottom. The connecting level could be scaled to that size and filled with miniscule monsters or be a normal dungeon level, putting the PCs at a severe disadvantage when encountering its residents.
6	Charge a toll. At a point along the stair's length, a barrier prevents further progress. In order to pass this blockade, the party must give up money, gems, magic, or some other precious belonging. The toll might be deposited into a special receptacle or simply vanish from the PCs' possession. A living or at least sentient toll collector may also be present at the barrier.
7	Are longer than they appear. Due to cunning construction or subtle magics, the stairs seem to descend a much shorter distance than they actually do, leading the party to believe they've only traveled down a single level when instead they've gone much, much further into the dungeon. A wise dwarf or divination magics might discern the truth, but it is far more likely the deception becomes apparent only when the party encounters their first fearsome monster on "the next level down" and finds it much more powerful than anticipated.
8	Collapse to form a slippery slide that plunges the party to a deeper level. Awaiting them at the bottom of the chute might be alerted guards, hungry beasts, or a wall of rusty, blood-stained spikes.
9	Siphon liquids away. For each step a PC takes on the stairs, a small portion of any liquids in their possession vanishes, sipped away by magical wards placed upon the staircase. Those that reach the bottom discover their waterskins are empty, their holy water missing, and their costly restorative potions gone. Parties that discover this draining effect before reaching the stair's bottom can turn around and avoid further liquid loss, but their magical elixirs might now have a limited duration or effect due to insufficient draughts.
10	Are one-way. Travels down the stairs can only go in a single direction. This might be caused by a concealed barrier that falls into place, blocking the stairs once the last member steps off them or be the result of repulsive magics that make it impossible to ascend the steps once the bottom is reached. One-way stairs are especially dangerous if the party used them to enter an unexplored level. With no easy retreat available, they have no hope of running from a superior foe.
11	Are statically charged. The stairs are covered in an unusual wooly material that generates static electricity. By the time the party reaches the bottom, each has become charged with static electricity of unusual strength. Party members touching metal or flesh discharge the electrical force, doing damage to themselves and others. A cunning party might be able to use this energy to their benefit, but so might other residents of the dungeon.
12	Are illusionary. Although seemingly solid, the stairs are nothing but a realistic hologram or illusionary magic. The first party member who steps upon them vanishes as they plummet down a shaft concealed by the false stairs. Depending on the source of the illusion, the remainder of the party might not realize what has occurred.
13	Have no visible means of support. Instead of being a solid staircase, each step floats independently in the air, held aloft by magical means. The steps might be secure or bob underfoot when weight is placed on them, possibly causing a careless traveler to fall. Some steps might be missing entirely, forcing the party to take desperate leaps across yawning gaps to make further progress down the stairs.
14	Lead somewhere utterly unexpected. Although unremarkable in appearance, those descending the steps find themselves in a location that could not reasonably be situated in the dungeon. Another plane of existence, a distant city, the mind of a powerful sorcerer, or a favorite fantasy tale of the referee are some possibilities. Exiting these realms may simply be a matter of ascending the stairs or could require more difficult means to escape.
15	Are intermittent. Although solid stone and otherwise normal, there are times when the stairs simply aren't there. An empty shaft might stand where the stairs should be, or there might not be anything at all occupying the space where the staircase typically is located. These periods of vanishing may be on a regular schedule or occur without warning. The fate of those on the steps when they vanish could be grim.
16	Are a monster. One of the strange subterranean creatures who have evolved the ability to mimic normal dungeon decoration has mutated further and can now replicate lengthy stretches of stonework. This monster currently disguises itself as a short flight of stairs down to an alcove or pit. Parties venturing down the step are in truth entering the beast's throat and are in for an unpleasant surprise.
17	Are musical. Stepping upon one or more steps causes a musical note to sound, reverberating down the stairwell. Each pipe organ-like note is perfectly tuned and deft footwork can cause intricate musical compositions to be played. These musical stairs might be due to a quirk of the dungeon's designer, a warning system, or the key to unlocking hidden mysteries. Perhaps when a specific tune is played a secret door opens or a magical effect occurs.
18	Warm metal objects. As the party descends the steps, any metal objects possessed by them gradually grow warmer, eventually becoming hot to the touch. PCs must discard these items or be burned by them. Native dungeon inhabitants not prone to using metal weapons and armor often lurk at the foot of the stairs to ambush the now unarmored and unarmed interlopers from the surface.
19	Record and replay images. The stairs possess the magical ability to record and reproduce visual "echoes" of any creature that uses them. These images might be replayed immediately or stored and repeated after a specific delay. Intelligent monsters might use the stairs' power to lure enemies into an ambush, while explorers unaware of the stairs' property might suddenly encounter their exact duplicates coming the other way upon returning from their expedition.
20	A secret treadmill. Walking down the staircase causes hidden machinery to turn, moving the stairs in place beneath the party's feet. So subtle is this effect the PCs are unlikely to detect it and may deduce that the stairs are endless. This effect works in both directions and unless deactivated can strand the party on the stairs permanently. An even more fiendish option is that the treadmill serves as a dynamo that generates power for a concealed trap, which is activated after sufficient power is produced.

IS FOR TRAPS

For more than one adventurer, the last thing they've heard on this side of the shroud is the soft "click" of a depressed flagstone or the sharp "snick" of a spring-loaded needle sliding home. They have run afoul of one of the myriad traps that guard the secrets of the dungeon. In order to protect the **Gold**, **Jewels**, and **Magic** secreted in the dungeon, many contraptions, both magic and mundane, have been placed to guard them. A dungeon without traps is like a house without **Books**: it lacks its very soul.

Traps come in countless forms, being limited only by the creativity and wealth of their creators. Some are minute and easy to overlook, only discovered when the attempt to open a locked chest goes awry. Others are of massive construction, bringing down the entire ceiling of a **Room** onto a hapless party that didn't follow the correct pattern on the checkered tile floor below. In between these extremes lies a plethora of perils: volleys of darts, spears rocketing from walls, gas- or water-filled **Rooms**, walls that suddenly clap together or grind slowly to seal one's doom, covered pits (with or without spikes), inward falling **Doors**, rolling rocks, showers of serpents, scything blades, clay jars filled with green slime that fall from above, harmful **Inscriptions**, poison-coated **Gold**, exploding **Jewels**, and even traps that look like traps but actually do no harm. The party must thread their way through these dangers if they wish to lay their hands upon the treasures that wait beyond.

THIRTY FIENDISH TRAPS

1	Poison needle.
2	Scything blade slashes at hands.
3	Fusillade of darts.
4	Spears spring from wall/floor.
5	Poison gas spews from object.
6	Cantilevered floor spills victim into pit/pool of acid/watery pit with aquatic monster.
7	Rocks/stone slab/loose bricks fall from above.
8	Portcullis descends, blocking exits/spearing those underneath.
9	Arrows/quarrels fired from concealment.
10	Room floods with water/acid/monstrous slime or ooze.
11	Walls of the room compact, squishing the party between them.
12	Ceiling descends – spikes may or may not protrude.
13	Spring-loaded flagstone launches victim into the air, splattering him against the ceiling.
14	Magical glyph or runes.
15	Fake trap – object bears false hints that it is trapped but is quite safe.
16	Magical ray strikes victim – turns to stone, searing heat, freezing cold, etc.
17	Room fills with poisonous gas.
18	Mundane object(s) – statue, furniture, etc. spring to life and attack.
19	Pendulum blades swing from the ceiling.
20	Trapdoor opens, dumping victim down a shaft – may lead to lower level, monster's den, or inflict falling damage.
21	Monster released from concealed pen into the room.
22	Object smeared with contact poison.
23	Rolling rock released to crush adventurers underneath.
24	Object filled with serpents, spiders, or other venomous vermin.
25	Massive stone slab seals the chamber – party may starve to death or another threat might be added.
26	Covered pit – with or without spikes.
27	Net/snare entangles victim and lifts him/her aloft.
28	Object covered with super-strength adhesive, possibly immobilizing the victim or encumbering him.
29	False treasure – object is a disguised monster.
30	Object teleports victim to random/pre-determined location.

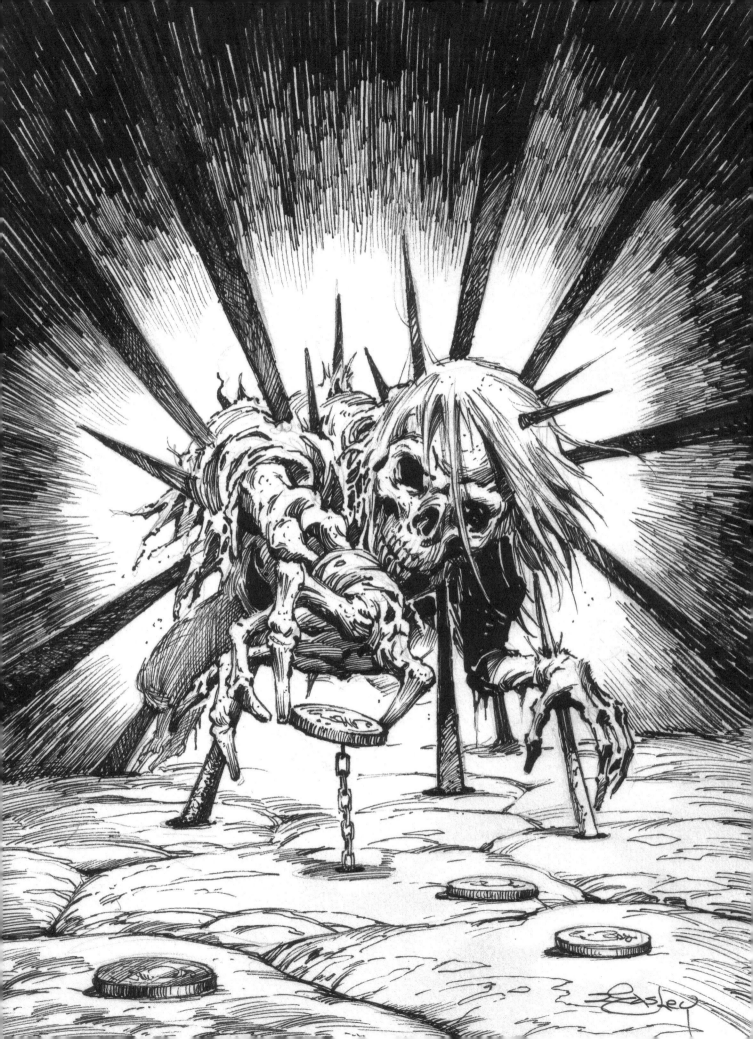

IS ALSO FOR TREASURE CHESTS

The sight of a massive chest standing in a dark corner after the last of his foes has fallen causes a weary adventurer's spirit to soar. Great treasures are deposited in such containers, supposedly safe and secure against greedy hands. In some cases, these treasure chests have only a flimsy lock protecting their contents, but often more formidable protections guard the glittering coins, sparkling gems, and potent magics they contain.

Although **Traps** are usually employed along with locks to keep treasure chests secure, it is sometimes the box itself that proves to be wealth's greatest guardian. From false bottoms to contact poisons to powerful enchantments laid upon the box, there is no shortage of alternate means to keep a treasure safe within a chest. Rarer and more dangerous are special varieties of chests that act as guardians, calling upon weird magics and cunning designs to thwart the most dedicated thief. If these security measures can be breached without destroying the box, the chest itself can be claimed and is commonly as valuable as the wealth it holds. Greedy merchants, paranoid potentates, and veteran adventurers seeking to protect their spoils pay large sums to acquire these unique treasure chests. The seller of such containers need beware, however. An unscrupulous purchaser may take steps to eliminate anyone with knowledge of the chest's defenses to better protect their wealth.

TWENTY-THREE RARE AND UNUSUAL TREASURE CHESTS

2d12	The chest is...
2	Inside another chest. Like a set of nesting dolls, one or more smaller chests reside inside the first. Each one is locked and trapped, requiring numerous keys or successfully larcenous skill tests to reach the final box that contains the treasure. Due to space limitations, the last chest is unlikely to contain much, but what it does hold will be highly valuable to warrant such security precautions.
3	Magnetized. Any would-be thief approaching the chest and bearing large amounts of steel is forcefully attracted to and becomes stuck to the heavy, iron container. The magnetic attraction is powerful enough that the PC cannot free himself unless he possesses abnormal strength. Attempts to pick the chest's lock or disable its trap through physical methods are doomed to fail as the thief's tools fly from his hand and become affixed to the chest. These chests usually contain non-ferrous treasures and are opened with ceramic, bone, or glass keys.
4	Invisible. The contents, however, are not, and neither is the needle or scything blade that guards the wealth. The treasure seems to mock those who would claim it. The trap's trigger and internal mechanisms are invisible, making disarming the trap a difficult task. A failed attempt to render the trap inactive is likely to set it off.
5	Covered with transparent and extremely strong glue. Coating one's hands in a common substance (soot, oil, water, etc.) prevents the glue from sticking, but only the chest's owner(s) know that trick. Adventurers with knowledge of dungeon monsters might assume the chest is actually one of those rare beasts that can mimic dungeon accoutrements.
6	Magically animated and will either fight or flee the party when approached. A special command word negates the animation, allowing the chest to be pilfered more easily, although other safeguards may still be in place.
7	Out of phase. The chest is clearly visible, but all attempts to touch it cause the PC's hands to pass through it as if it were an illusion or hologram. A special pair of gloves (usually secreted nearby) or powerful plane-crossing magic is needed to access the chest.
8	Affixed to the ceiling with magic or adhesive. This tactic is generally employed by exceptionally tall races or those who can walk on walls. Upside-down thieves attempting to detect traps or pick the lock suffer penalties for doing so in an unusual position.
9	Spell-proof. Powerful adventurers become accustomed to opening even the most stubborn or trapped chests from a safe distance with the appropriate magical spells. This chest is warded against these magics. Some forms of spell-proofing transform and reflect such breaching magics, changing them into magical fire bursts or lightning strikes directed back at the caster.
10	Throws a glamour upon its contents. Any object placed in the chest assumes a valuable appearance. Mundane items seem bejeweled, copper coins appear to be platinum, and glass baubles look like rare gemstones. This magical glamour lasts for a short time once the object is removed from the chest, but unless the looter dawdles in bagging the loot, it's unlikely he'll notice its true worth until after he's exited the dungeon. The real valuables are kept in a false bottom or other hidden location in or near the chest.
11	Fashioned to resemble a stone block. The chest is placed in a cavity in a wall, making it seem to be an ordinary dungeon building block. Only careful searching reveals the slight depressions in the stone that act as handholds for pulling the chest out and accessing its contents.
12	Formed from a giant creature's skull. The skull's upper portion is sawed off and reattached with stout hinges. Metal places are attached to the eye sockets and nasal cavity to prevent access through those channels. Many such skull chests are animated undead as well, keyed to attack looters.
13	Inside a creature. Powerful wizards and mad inventors enjoy hiding their wealth inside one of their creations. The torso of an iron golem is the perfect place to build or hide a treasure chest. Not only is it secret, but it has powerful protection without the need for locks and traps. Biological guardians are also used, but the means to deposit or retrieve one's wealth is much less convenient.
14	Restricts withdrawals. The chest is enchanted so that only a single item can be removed and replaced each day. Attempts to withdraw more than one item causes a force field to appear across the mouth of the chest, preventing access to its contents until the following day. One item can be placed in the chest; the barrier allows it to pass through, but blocks anything trying to exit the chest. These chests are typically locked in place to prevent the entire chest from being carried off.
15	Disintegrates its contents. The chest is used to store sensitive materials better destroyed completely lest they fall into the wrong hands. Unless opened with the correct key, magical coils inside the chest emit disintegrating rays that vaporize its contents. Paranoid wizards often store their spellbooks inside such chests, provided they have a spare set secreted somewhere else.
16	Vampiric. This chest has no visible lock but is bloodstained and has curious funnel-shaped holes upon its lid. To open a vampiric chest, blood from either the opener or a sacrifice must be spilled over it. The funnels absorb the vital fluid, unlocking the chest.
17	A mirror. This chest can only be seen inside a mirror or other reflective surface. The person wishing to access its contents must manipulate the chest's reflection, drawing its treasures out of the looking glass. When locked and trapped, attempts to physically bypass these security measures are penalized due to the difficulties in working on the chest in its mirrored, reversed stated.
18	Opens under certain conditions. The chest only opens when specific conditions apply. Some are time-locked, opening at set periods during the day, week, or month. Others only open in darkness or under the light of the new moon. These chests are commonly placed in locations that make meeting the condition difficult but not entirely inconvenient to the owner.
19	Battery locked. Several odd tubes, crystals, and wires wind their way across the surface of the chest. The box will not open unless an electrical charge is fist applied to the chest, typically through a magic spell or wand. Attempts to bash open the chest result in the thief being electrocuted by the container's power system.
20	A "music box." These chests are crafted from fine, but unnaturally strong crystal that vibrates when exposed to musical tones. A specific note or series of notes needs to be played near the chest to open the container. Keys to music boxes are specially tuned whistles or other simple musical instruments that can be easily carried without attracting attention.
21	A "toy box." A toy box chest can refer to either a toy designed to hold hidden valuables or an actual toy box containing treasure. Secret toy boxes can be anything from a doll's house with an extra-dimensional space for treasure to a rocking horse with a concealed container in its back. Actual toy box treasure chests are typically found in the lairs of demonic children, regressive madmen, or in the bedchambers of prepubescent princes and princesses.
22	Disguised as a chamber pot. The chest is a wooden crate or ceramic pot befouled with waste and stinking. Its contents are buried beneath a layer of filth that discourages digging around in the chest. Any PC pulling the treasure free from the bodily waste it contains risks contracting a disease if the proper precautions are not taken.
23	Gaseous. The chest and all its contents exist in a gaseous but immobile state. A solid lock hangs in the mist and unlocking the chest with the proper key causes the container and its riches to revert to a solid state.
24	Greed-cursed. Covered in macabre carvings of warring creatures, the chest casts a baleful curse if two or more persons are present when it is opened. The curse causes anyone glimpsing the chest's contents to be overcome with irresistible greed and the desire for sole ownership of its riches. Cursed individuals will attack to kill anyone else staking a claim on the chest's contents.

IS FOR UNDEAD

When all that is true and good has fled the mortal shell of what once was a man, sometimes something lingers behind. Born of hatred, fear, and hunger, this grim spark of sentience animates what should be moldering quietly beneath the earth. Having crawled from dusty sarcophagi, hoary barrows, and the too-loosely sealed niches of sepulchers, these undead things walk in the darkness below.

The undead are stark reminders of the fate that may await the incautious adventurer. Once they too lived, breathed, and loved, only to succumb to this unholy state. Many of the undead the party encounters have the ability to pass their doomed condition on to those who fall beneath their attacks. And it is when the foes that the party confronts were once cherished loved ones, or stalwart boon companions, that the true horrors of the undead bloom to fruition.

Undead enemies are free from even the token constraints of ecology or reason. Needing neither air nor food, and possessing the patience of the dead, the undead can lurk still and silent within the dungeon, awaiting their next victim. They can rise from long-dead bones, burst from walled-up cavities, or materialize from the stones surrounding the adventurers. They remind the party that the cleric in their ranks is not merely a convenient walking first-aid kit, but a holy warrior who wields the power of the divine. Lastly, powerful undead, such as vampires, liches, death knights, and magic-wielding mummy pharaohs make perfect nemeses for the party; patient beyond death, and uncaring of human suffering or peril.

2d8 Roll	UNIQUE UNDEAD ENCOUNTERS
2	A vampire lurks in the dungeon, feeding off the denizens of many levels. Adventurers might be able to unite monsters against it.
3	Two ghostly warriors constantly reenact the duel that killed them both. Will resent anyone who intrudes upon their eternal fight.
4	The mummies of the dungeon's original work crew, killed to protect the dungeon's secrets.
5	An angry poltergeist haunts an armory, hurling dangerous weapons at any who enter.
6	A pack of aristocratic and well-mannered ghouls who invite the party to dinner — one way or the other.
7	Headless skeletons prowl the dungeon. Will serve whoever returns their skulls to them.
8	Zombies and skeletons infested with giant centipedes, bore worms, or other vermin.
9	A dozen zombies drowned and sealed in a capped well.
10	A magical mishap destroyed a wizard and his apprentices, burning their shadows into the walls of their workroom. These malevolent shadows retain a ghastly sentience.
11	The wights of sacred guardians are entombed in the walls of the dungeon, springing forth from the crumbling bricks to surprise the unwary.
12	Party of dead adventurers continues their foray into the dungeon, unaware that they are dead.
13	The wailing spirit of an elven noblewoman sweeps through the hallways, seeking the deaths of all who remind her of her treacherous lover.
14	A spectral funeral procession regularly appears in the hallways of the dungeon.
15	A flesh golem, accompanied by the wraiths of those whose parts were used to construct it, lurks in the dungeon depths.
16	An insane lich composer working to complete his masterpiece composition.

Even the bravest adventurer will blanch with fear when confronted by the dark, silent waters that sometime collect in dungeons. Whether these bodies of water are subterranean lakes, stagnant rain that has seeped from above for centuries, or the result of underground springs leaking into the dungeon, all are dreaded by those from the sunlit lands above. Who knows what lurks in those black seas, watching from just below the surface

A Dozen Underwater Dungeon Dangers

D12 The party faces...

1   A patch of water tainted by a flooded alchemical laboratory. Anyone passing through the magically polluted wate must make a saving throw or be affected by the alchemical waters. Beneficial effects may occur (healing, sup strength, etc.), but the chance of more hazardous changes (poisoning, polymorph, etc.) is equally likely.

2   Traps of increased lethality when triggered underwater. While fire-based traps will likely be ineffective, ones employi lightning have an increased area of effect or higher saving throw, while cold-based traps encase their targets spheres of ice, leading to swift suffocation.

3   Unless the party is scrupulously cautious, venturing underwater quickly destroys magical tomes and scrolls, robbi the party of useful magic and spellcasters the ability to recover expended spells.

4   Powerful currents difficult to detect in the darkened waters. A strong undertow—created by magical forces underground topography—sweeps PCs off their feet and carries them into the dungeon depths. They may or may end up in a space where breathable air exists once the current has weakened.

5   Some scholars maintain that life originated in the world's waters. What might be breeding down in the lightless se underneath the earth, many of which are steeped in magical energies? Underwater dungeon environments are perfect place to introduce mutated lifeforms, living fossils, or weirder creatures.

6   A vast flooded crypt complex spawns new forms of the un-dead. While the aquatic ghoul is a staple in some fantasy RPGs, why not waterlogged mummies (safely non-flammable) or vampires who are now immune to running water and can summon schools of flesh-eating cave fish or giant albino crawdads instead of wolves and bats?

Dealing with watery hazards in the dungeon force adventurers to overcome concerns beyond hostile creatures. Will they have to remove their heavy armor? Do they know how to swim? How deep is the water and will the party's dwarves and halflings need to be carried by their taller comrades? A single misstep in even the shallowest waters is enough to soak a party's entire supply of torches, stranding them in darkness with foes all around them. It is little wonder that nothing strikes fear into the hearts of experienced adventurers—and their players—quite like a stretch of flooded dungeon in need of crossing. Under such circumstances, it's all too easy for an adventurer to get in over his head!

A Dozen Underwater Dungeon Dangers Continued

D12   The party faces...

7   Footing is much more hazardous in the flooded dungeon. A party wandering through waist-deep water while clad in heavy armor might suddenly plunge into an open pit and drown or wander off a ledge into deeper waters, wherein live much larger monsters than the supposedly shallow depth might suggest.

8   Treasure becomes harder to recover. Caches of heavy gold coins require magic or ingenious means of buoyancy to bring them to the surface. Coins and jewelry long submerged might become tarnished or discolored, making it difficult to gauge their true value while underwater.

9   Aquatic assailants strike from all directions underwater. Parties must worry about ambushes from above and below as well as lateral directions. A party of aquatic goblins might wait in the darkness near a submerged room's ceiling, attacking the less armored PCs in the party's middle ranks such as wizards. The writhing tentacles of a dungeon squid could strike from the depths of a chasm or open pit, dragging adventurers to their doom.

10   Spells and effects negating magic become much more lethal in a flooded dungeon. A party adventuring through the submerged chambers, thanks to a water-breathing potion or a similar magic item, suddenly finds themselves drowning when their sorcery fails.

11   Common dungeon hazards taking on new underwater forms. Green slime, oozes, and pudding may become unrecognizable spheres, their true nature only revealed when the party gets too close. Ambush predators like lurkers above or trappers might become aggressive predators, swimming through the water on manta ray-like wings.

12   New aquatic dungeon hazards that replace the classic ones. Imagine weeds that dissolve flesh and metal like acidic slime or freshwater snails that burrow into an unfortunate victim's flesh like rot grubs!

IS FOR VERMIN

Scuttling, wriggling, and crawling through the unlit depths, vermin thrive in the damp confines of the dungeon. Some are merely slightly larger specimens of their surface-dwelling kin, while others are true monsters in both size and temperament. The dungeon is a nasty place and its vermin inhabitants even nastier.

When not encountering **Kobolds**, beginning parties of adventurers commonly earn their early experience points through the extermination of vermin. Giant rats, centipedes, spiders, and beetles are often encountered on the upper levels of the dungeon. This trope is so ingrained into the genre of fantasy role-playing that it has escaped into the MMORPG, earning the nomenclature "yard trash." As the party delves deeper, the bugs and vermin get bigger and more vicious. Spiders of Shelob-sized caliber await the explorers, centipedes become megalopedes, and beetles possess strange properties such as squirting oil or exploding and popping abdomens that unleash caustic chemicals onto those who wish to eradicate them.

Vermin are despised by adventurers. Many are put off by their large size or an ingrained phobia of things with too many legs. Most adventurers learn to hate these squirmy things for the same reason that some referees gleefully include them: they can range from mere annoyance to outright fatal opponents, yet they never have any treasure.

2d6 Roll	RANDOM VERMIN CHALLENGES TO PLAGUE THE ADVENTURERS
2	A nest of pack rats that carry off loose gear and treasure, taking it back to their lair of small tunnels in the dungeon's walls.
3	The adventurers encounter a type of vermin that possesses, either by natural mutation or magical experimentation, the traits of two or more kinds of vermin. Examples include spiders that glow like fire beetles, rats with poisonous stingers, or centipedes that spin webs.
4	A gifted humanoid musician has perfected a tune that summons large numbers of vermin to serve him.
5	An army of harmless vermin (mites, lice, chiggers, etc.) infest the clothing and armor of the adventurers. The vermin must be exterminated before the articles can be worn again properly.
6	A horde of rats carries a particularly virulent form of disease, either increasing the chance of transmitting the disease through wounds or infecting the victim with a more deadly, possibly even magical, disease.
7	A large herd of fire beetles is maintained by one of the dungeon's humanoid tribes for food and their natural luminescent properties. This herd is tended by bands of "beetle-pokes" who guard their herd against rustlers.
8	One level of the dungeon is inhabited by giant spiders that possess a genius intellect. They have transformed the entire level into a cunning trap that guides prey into their clutches.
9	A twitching body is found sprawled on the floor of a room. While apparently still possessing life, it is actually a corpse infested with lively vermin.
10	A colony of giant ants has honeycombed a section of the dungeon. They have also unearthed a vein of gold which they mine and store in the royal chamber, where it is defended by soldiers and the queen alike.
11	A swarm of normal sized flesh-eating beetles infest a forgotten tomb located within the dungeon. Although harmless in small numbers, they can strip an entire group of adventurers to the bone when found in such great numbers.
12	After a rest period, one of the party reaches into his backpack to retrieve some item only to feel the nasty — possibly poisonous — bite of a centipede, spider, or rat which had sought shelter within the dark confines of that container.

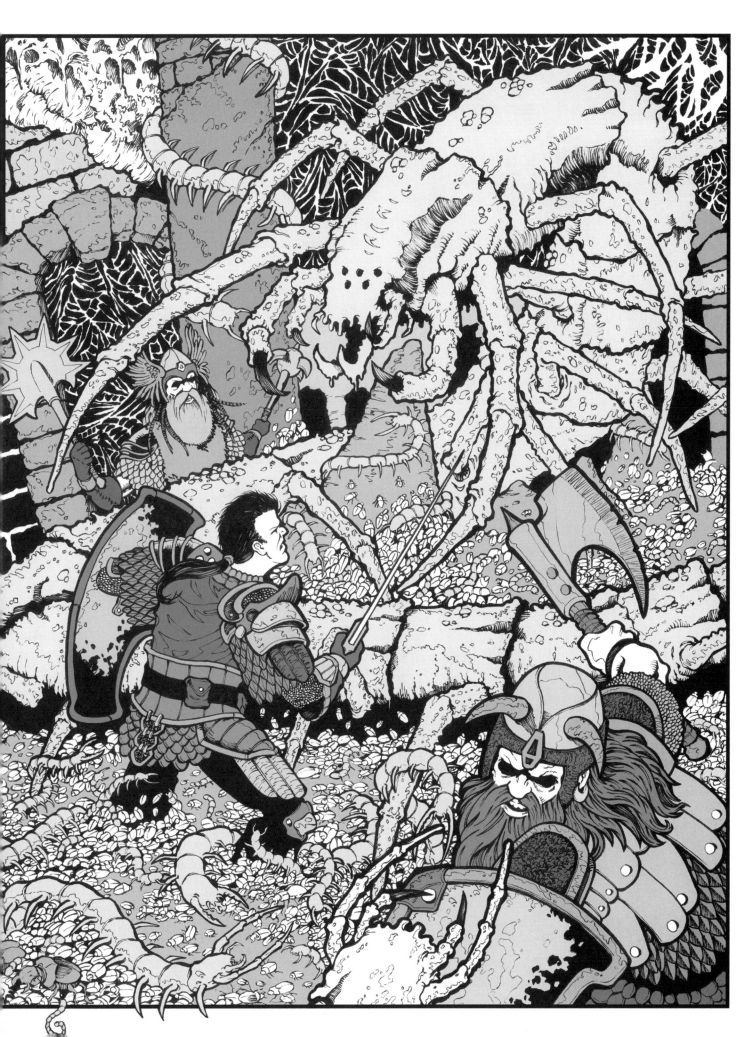

IS ALSO FOR VEGETATION

The lightless subterranean depths seem ill-suited for greenery. Unyielding stone and the absence of the sun thwart the attempts of grass, flower, and tree to take root and thrive. The dungeon is where **Fungi** grow, at home in the darkness.

Yet there are numerous accounts of adventurers encountering verdant growths of green in the most unlikely places of the chthonic realms. Greenhouses lit by artificial suns are found in mage's lairs. Albino plants, drawing life from weird subterranean radiations, grow in underworld groves. Hanging plants that thrive on strange substances decorate hypogeal cities. Mad cave druids cultivate crops with their natural divinity.

Vegetation is the staff of life of the surface world, the stuff upon which greater creatures feed. In the deep dungeons, however, this is not necessarily the norm. An unwary adventure might find himself the prey of the bizarre plant life flowering away from the sun. The most experienced adventurers seek out alchemists and sages to purchase special herbicides to protect themselves when encountering subterranean greenery. Some of these expensive elixirs even work

FOURTEEN FUNKY FLOWERS AND PLANTS

D14	The vegetation is…
1	A nature mimic, reproducing any sound made in its presence with trumpet-like blossoms. Motion near the plant activates this re-play response. Some subterranean races use the plant's properties to pass along messages, as an alarm system, or even record sonic attacks in order to injure or kill trespassers.
2	Stimulated by energy sources, causing sudden, spontaneous growth. Heat, light, cold, even breathing causes the plant to abruptly grow ten times its size, entangling those nearby, blocking passages, or otherwise causing difficulties to the ones responsible for the growth spurt.
3	Fed by uncommon sources of sustenance. The plant draws life from blood, magma, spell slots, intelligence, magical potions, or another unusual substance. It possesses an animal cunning to help acquire its preferred food source.
4	Parasitic and can take root in other living creatures. The plant feeds off its host and can subconsciously influence its actions to better benefit the plant.
5	The resting place for a sorcerer's intellect and personality. The magician either became entrapped in the plant when a magical experiment went awry or willingly passed his mind into the greenery in an attempt to prolong his life or avoid enemies. The transference may be permanent or it could be reversible, assuming a new potential subject for transference comes along.
6	The last living specimen from antediluvian times. Wiped out elsewhere in the world, the plant has survived only in this one location. Druids might be moved to reseed the plant and help the endangered species to thrive once more. But what if the plant possesses properties hazardous to life on the planet and was driven to near-extinction for a reason?
7	The herald of an alien invasion. A race from another planet or dimension is keen on invading the PCs' home world and is using the plant as a scout to gather intelligence. The invaders can hear and see all activity around the plant and may decide the PCs are either useful patsies for their plans or potential obstacles in need of removal.
8	An oracle possessing roots that extend into both the past and the future. If communication can be established with the plant—likely through the use of magic—questioners can learn about events from long ago or yet to occur. The plant's knowledge may be, ahem, rooted in a single place making its knowledge localized or its tendrils might extend throughout the multiverse.
9	Filled with sap possessing odd properties. The sap could be poisonous, medicinal, adhesive, sentient, able to reproduce the effects of magic potions, or have other unexpected benefits or drawbacks as determined by the game master.
10	A repository of lost lore. Centuries ago, some sage encouraged the vegetation to grow in topiary fashion, forming secret symbols and powerful glyphs embedded with eldritch wisdom. Anyone deciphering the meaning of the plant's twisted boughs and branches gains access to these mysteries.
11	The source of an energy field that negates racial advantages. Creatures lose their infravision, find their inherent magical powers fail, or otherwise cannot access their superhuman heritage. Insular communities of savage humans deep in the underworld plant this vegetation around their settlements.
12	A special component in religious rites. When burned as an incense or fermented into sacred beverages, the plant grants the rite's attendees insight into the will of the gods. Whether this is actually a divine conduit or simply a power hallucinogenic is left to the game master's discretion.
13	A natural magical amplifier or dampener. All magical power used in the plant's vicinity is ether double or tripled in intensity, or fails outright. The plant might continue to affect magic after being uprooted or harvested depending on the game master's desires.
14	Part of a druid's scheme to bring balance to the underworld. The plant hails from a plane of good and the druid planted it here in the dungeon to counterbalance evil's grip on the subterranean realms. If the plant is harmed, the druid's anger is roused and the defilers find themselves under siege by chthonic forces of nature.

IS FOR WEIRD

In addition to the strange powers and perils of **Altars**, **Statues**, **Rooms**, and **Pools**, other forms of the weird and the strange await the adventurers as they explore the deep dungeon. These weird events and items color the atmosphere of the depths, reminding the party that they are no longer in the realm of reason and common sense. They have entered the Underworld and should not expect things to behave in a rational manner.

The weird of the dungeon are usually quiet and unsettling things. They are not events like the sudden alteration of the laws of gravity or the discovery that the **Hallways** are actually the digestive tract of some gigantic beast. These things have their place in the dungeon but are more **Zowie!** than weird.

No, the weird in the dungeon is a small patch of moss that seems to sob like a frightened child. It is a pool of congealed blood on the ceiling of a corridor. It is the sound of strange flutes piping up from the depths below, accompanied by the laughter of ladies. It is the smell of lilac perfume in the air, when all around is dust and decay. Weird is not overtly dangerous or threatening; it is unnerving and spine-tingling. It is the reminder that the dungeon asks many **Questions** and it is up to the adventurers to try and unravel those mysteries. When done right, a weird event or encounter may be more memorable that the greatest fight the adventurers survive and may lay the seeds for future adventurers or attempts into the dungeon.

PERPLEXING THINGS AND EVENTS OF A WEIRD NATURE

1	A preserved humanoid head encased in a fluid-filled glass jar or bottle.
2	A clock with occult symbols on its face and more hands than normal. Clock may run faster or slower than normal, or even backwards.
3	A trail of footprints which ends abruptly in the middle of a room or hallway.
4	A statue or painting that seems to weep tears. Tears may be normal salty water or of a more unusual nature (blood, bile, wine, etc.).
5	A normal animal, one seemingly out of place in a dungeon such as a cat, deer, ferret, or canary, is occasionally spotted by the adventurers. The animal only appears at a distance and easily eludes any attempts to pursue or capture it.
6	A chamber which seems to have recently been subject to a passing rain or snow storm.
7	A set of stairs that ends abruptly at a blank stone wall.
8	An elegant meal is laid out on a banquet table. The food is warm and partially eaten but there is no sign of the diners. It is as if they suddenly left their meal with no trace of where they went or why.
9	A mirror that reflects the images of people not present in the room.
10	A discoloration of the stones in a dungeon wall resembles the silhouette of a man. He may appear to be in a bold posture or cowed in fear. The implications and cause of this discoloration are left to the referee.
11	A cloud of glowing dust motes floats in the air in some difficult to reach place (in a high balcony, on the far side of a deep chasm, or atop a stone pillar).
12	Periodically, the adventurers hear the faint sound of a song echoing through the dungeon. Sometimes it sounds like an ancient elvish lament about a lover who has gone far away, while other times it is a simple child's nursery rhyme, one known by all the adventurers from their youth.

AN A-TO-Z REFERENCE FOR CLASSIC DUNGEON DESIGN 75

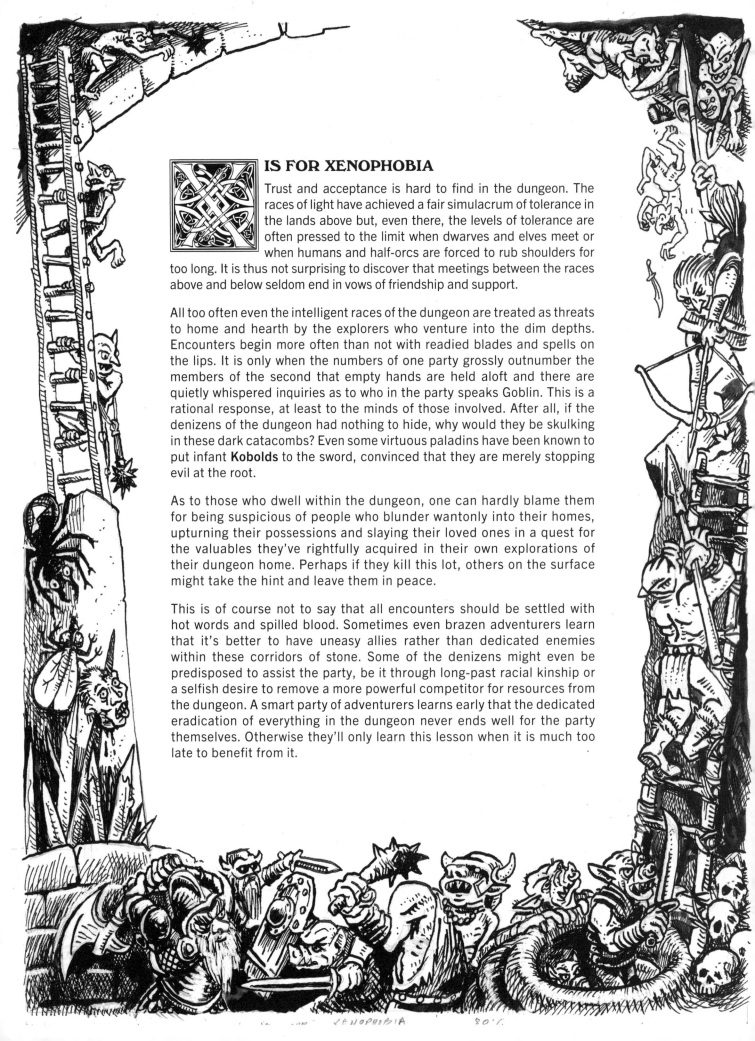

IS FOR XENOPHOBIA

Trust and acceptance is hard to find in the dungeon. The races of light have achieved a fair simulacrum of tolerance in the lands above but, even there, the levels of tolerance are often pressed to the limit when dwarves and elves meet or when humans and half-orcs are forced to rub shoulders for too long. It is thus not surprising to discover that meetings between the races above and below seldom end in vows of friendship and support.

All too often even the intelligent races of the dungeon are treated as threats to home and hearth by the explorers who venture into the dim depths. Encounters begin more often than not with readied blades and spells on the lips. It is only when the numbers of one party grossly outnumber the members of the second that empty hands are held aloft and there are quietly whispered inquiries as to who in the party speaks Goblin. This is a rational response, at least to the minds of those involved. After all, if the denizens of the dungeon had nothing to hide, why would they be skulking in these dark catacombs? Even some virtuous paladins have been known to put infant **Kobolds** to the sword, convinced that they are merely stopping evil at the root.

As to those who dwell within the dungeon, one can hardly blame them for being suspicious of people who blunder wantonly into their homes, upturning their possessions and slaying their loved ones in a quest for the valuables they've rightfully acquired in their own explorations of their dungeon home. Perhaps if they kill this lot, others on the surface might take the hint and leave them in peace.

This is of course not to say that all encounters should be settled with hot words and spilled blood. Sometimes even brazen adventurers learn that it's better to have uneasy allies rather than dedicated enemies within these corridors of stone. Some of the denizens might even be predisposed to assist the party, be it through long-past racial kinship or a selfish desire to remove a more powerful competitor for resources from the dungeon. A smart party of adventurers learns early that the dedicated eradication of everything in the dungeon never ends well for the party themselves. Otherwise they'll only learn this lesson when it is much too late to benefit from it.

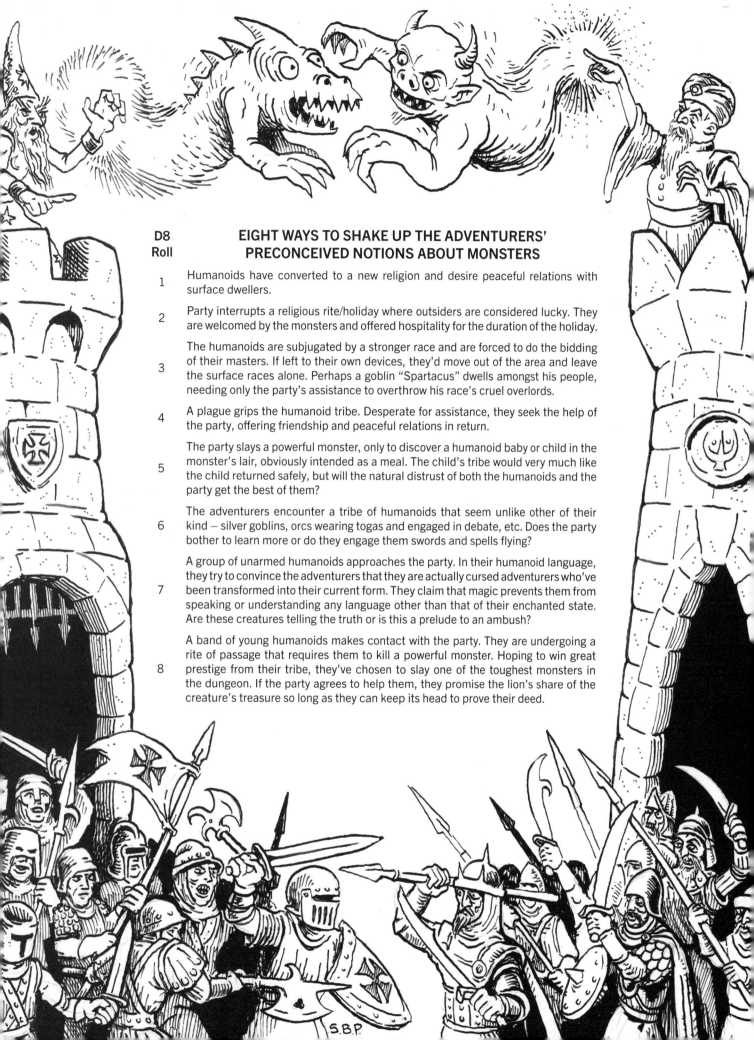

EIGHT WAYS TO SHAKE UP THE ADVENTURERS' PRECONCEIVED NOTIONS ABOUT MONSTERS

D8 Roll

1 Humanoids have converted to a new religion and desire peaceful relations with surface dwellers.

2 Party interrupts a religious rite/holiday where outsiders are considered lucky. They are welcomed by the monsters and offered hospitality for the duration of the holiday.

3 The humanoids are subjugated by a stronger race and are forced to do the bidding of their masters. If left to their own devices, they'd move out of the area and leave the surface races alone. Perhaps a goblin "Spartacus" dwells amongst his people, needing only the party's assistance to overthrow his race's cruel overlords.

4 A plague grips the humanoid tribe. Desperate for assistance, they seek the help of the party, offering friendship and peaceful relations in return.

5 The party slays a powerful monster, only to discover a humanoid baby or child in the monster's lair, obviously intended as a meal. The child's tribe would very much like the child returned safely, but will the natural distrust of both the humanoids and the party get the best of them?

6 The adventurers encounter a tribe of humanoids that seem unlike other of their kind – silver goblins, orcs wearing togas and engaged in debate, etc. Does the party bother to learn more or do they engage them swords and spells flying?

7 A group of unarmed humanoids approaches the party. In their humanoid language, they try to convince the adventurers that they are actually cursed adventurers who've been transformed into their current form. They claim that magic prevents them from speaking or understanding any language other than that of their enchanted state. Are these creatures telling the truth or is this a prelude to an ambush?

8 A band of young humanoids makes contact with the party. They are undergoing a rite of passage that requires them to kill a powerful monster. Hoping to win great prestige from their tribe, they've chosen to slay one of the toughest monsters in the dungeon. If the party agrees to help them, they promise the lion's share of the creature's treasure so long as they can keep its head to prove their deed.

Y IS FOR YELLOW

In the lands above, the shade of yellow is one associated with happy circumstances and pleasant days. Yellow is the color of dazzling sunlight, of swaying daffodils in the breeze, or is the tint of a true love's hair. It conjures up images of children playing on bright spring days and the taste of succulent fruits. In the realms below, however, the color yellow has grimmer associations.

In those dank catacombs, yellows come not in bright, cheerful hues, but in faded tinctures of age and rot. It is a sickly shade, calling to mind craven fear, shattering madness, and the unstoppable march to the grave. It is found in decaying texts and grimoires, their pages having yellowed with the passage of untold ages. It colors the rotted bones of the dead, turning them from bleached clean purity to the tone of an old man's teeth. Once-fine silk and lace clothes have faded to a dirty yellow tint in the dungeon's dank climate. Even the sheen of **Gold** is reduced to an unsettling dim yellow, rather than one gleaming and pristine.

Hideous denizens of the dungeons are also of this hue. From the fatal yellow mold, to the yellow musk creeper and its zombie-like creations, to the orange-yellow coloration of the ochre jelly, there are no good and clean yellows beneath the earth. For referees and players well acquainted with the works of Chambers, Lovecraft, and Derleth, the color yellow is an all too potent reminder of the King in Yellow, the wearer of the Pallid Mask, and the madness-inducing Yellow Sign. Players acquainted with older classic horror works are sure to recall Charlotte Perkins Gilman's "The Yellow Wallpaper," and the madness that accompanies that tale.

Yellow was once a more sinister hue than we consider it now. A clever referee will try to use this older association to — ahem — *color* his dungeon deep.

SIX SINISTER USES OF THE COLOR YELLOW

D6 Roll	
1	Deep in the dungeon, the adventurers surprise a group of cultists who conceal their identities with yellow robes and masks. When defeated, they are revealed to be common folk from the nearby town. Those taken alive reveal only they await the coming of "the king." What does this portend?
2	A mural depicting a cheerful and green land is painted upon the wall. With lush forests and verdant fields, all seems well. But as the adventurers move about, they notice that, when viewed from another angle, an unsettling hue of yellow seems to pervade the once-green landscape. On closer inspection, it seems this yellow plague originates from a castle/tower/monastery/etc. in the middle of the land. This structure is the very same one that the party is now exploring!
3	Raggedly thin, feral-looking humanoids infest a section of the dungeon. Their skin has grown a pallid yellow and become scaly and flaked. Something is affecting them, giving them strange abilities and powerful resistances. Whatever could be behind such a hideous mutation?
4	A dusty skeleton sits atop a throne in a dusty chamber, its once-fine garments now yellow and rotted with age. One bony arm is fused into rigidity and points languidly to a section of floor before it. Silence fills the air as if the chamber itself holds its breath in anticipation.
5	A triggered pressure plate causes the hallway to fill with a cloud of yellow gas. Roiling and billowing as if alive, the cloud moves quickly towards the party, threatening to engulf them.
6	A thick tome sits atop a pedestal, its yellowed pages open to reveal strange writing. Study of this tome will allow a spell caster to learn some new spell or prayer of unique power, provided that they are able to confront the hideous truths revealed in the book without succumbing to the madness such knowledge instills upon the reader.

MULLEN

IS FOR ZOWIE!

The Zowie! is related to the **Weird**, but where the weird is subtle and quiet, the zowie! is grandiose, memorable, and breathtaking. It is a feature or features that the adventurers will never fail to mention in the tales of their exploits — a memorable discovery that separates one particular dungeon from all the other subterranean complexes the party has explored.

Most dungeons possess at least one or two zowies!, but — like any good thing — quantity does not always equal quality. Too many wondrous things quickly cause them to lose their impact, rendering them merely implausible and tiresome. To combat this, the referee should limit his zowies! to one or fewer per level. In a pinch, more things weird can be added to spice things up, but the zowie! should be kept to small doses.

Examples of possible zowies! are: a vast, barren stone bridge that arcs over a river of molten lava; an underground forest comprised of crystalline trees; a gigantic cavern that houses a town built upon a stone platform, which is suspended from the ceiling by titanic chains; or a humongous book the size of a house, in which the names of all the adventurers to have entered the dungeon have been written. The dungeon itself could even be the zowie! The old TSR module *S3 - Expedition to the Barrier Peaks* is a classic example of this, as would be a dungeon that actually is the body of a dead god lying sprawled across a barren wasteland.

D20 Roll	TWENTY RANDOM ZOWIES! TABLE
1	"The Infernal Machine"
2	A tree with leaves of precious gold and silver.
3	A massive water-wheel that powers the dungeon's traps.
4	An empty suit of titanic plate mail.
5	A casino/gambling house run by monsters.
6	A crystal ziggurat that houses a giant beating heart at its center.
7	A gallery that bears statues in the likenesses of the adventurers.
8	A rustic village and its inhabitants all carved from living stone.
9	An orrery or model of the Cosmic Wheel.
10	A humongous cesspit inhabited by a congress of wise neo-otyughs.
11	The tomb of a dead demi-god.
12	A bottomless chamber filled with mist.
13	The purple worm graveyard where ancient worms go to die.
14	"The Parliament of Ghosts"
15	The rusting remains of a '57 Chevy.
16	Rows of vats containing the featureless forms of humanoids floating in liquid.
17	An abandoned wharf set on the shores of a sunless sea.
18	A series of Teslatrons spitting sparks and bolts of electricity.
19	"The Mother of All Puddings"
20	A wooly mammoth or other extinct beast encased in a block of ice.

ENTER →